Crossing Ocean Parkway

CROSSING

OCEAN

PARKWAY

Readings by an Italian American Daughter

Marianna De Marco Torgovnick

THE UNIVERSITY OF CHICAGO PRESS

Chicago and London

The University of Chicago Press, Chicago 60637
The University of Chicago Press, Ltd., London
©1994 by Marianna De Marco Torgovnick
All rights reserved. Published 1994
Printed in the United States of America

03 02 01 99 98 97 96 95 94   1 2 3 4 5

ISBN: 0-226-80829-7 (cloth)

"On Being White, Female, and Born in Bensonhurst" first appeared in *Partisan Review,*
vol. LVII, no. 3 (1990). "Slasher Stories" first appeared in *New Formations* (Summer
1992). *"The Godfather* as the World's Most Typical Novel" was published originally in
SAQ (Spring 1988); and "The Politics of the 'We'" was first printed in *SAQ* (Winter
1992). The versions which appear in this book have been revised.

Library of Congress Cataloging-in-Publication Data

Torgovnick, Marianna, 1949-
Crossing Ocean Parkway: readings by an Italian American daughter
/ Marianna De Marco Torgovnick
     p. cm.
   Includes bibliographical references.
   1. American literature--Italian American authors--History and
criticism. 2. Italian Americans--New York (N.Y.)--Social life and
customs. 3. Bensonhurst (New York, N.Y.)--Social life and customs.
4. Italian American women--Biography. 5. Italian Americans in
literature. 6. Torgovnick, Marianna, 1949- . I. Title.
PS153.I8T67   1994
810.9'851--dc20   94-14355
                                                      CIP

Contents

Preface

I am an Italian American woman married to a Jewish man—a classic New York mixed marriage. I know that Jews and Italian Americans go together as naturally as pizza and bagels fit into the American diet; in fact, as immigrants, they shared neighborhoods, jobs, and experiences. Yet accounts of life in the United States by Italian Americans are rare while many Jews, and especially Jewish men, have recorded the drama of moving up and out: Henry Roth, Philip Roth, Irving Howe, Vivian Gornick, Woody Allen, and others. Italian Americans are famous for many things—their food, their savvy in Northeastern politics, their celebrities, and their Mafia—but they are not usually known as writers. When they are, their writings usually either don't show their ethnicity (Don De Lillo) or bypass the Italian American experience for Italy itself (Luigi Barzini, Barbara Grizzuti Harrison). Even Gay Talese's *Unto the Sons* takes a detour to Calabria after its first one hundred pages and does not return to the U.S. until Talese has stopped writing in the first person. As his title implies, like many Italian American men, Talese is blind to the daughters' point of view.

Well into the second and third generations, most Italian Americans did not think about literature or writing. As Mario

Puzo observes in *The Godfather Papers,* they came from an illiterate culture, in which learning was the property of the *padroni,* the "big shots," and considered a useless and even dangerous thing for ordinary people. Most Italian Americans encouraged their sons to take pragmatic jobs with set salaries; they encouraged their daughters to marry. But times have changed, and so have Italian Americans.

Not so long ago, the following things would have been unthinkable for Italian Americans: being nominated for Vice President, serving on the Supreme Court, holding a cabinet post, running major corporations. But now all have come to pass. Increasingly, one sees *paesani* and *paesane* being interviewed on TV as newsmakers. I feel especially interested in the *paesane,* who (like me) often sport last names that aren't Italian.

The essays in this book are written from my special cultural situation: that of a female Italian American professor of English who lives in North Carolina and writes about American society. Teaching at Duke, I sometimes feel that ethnicity makes no difference—that universities have made me simply part of "the educated class." Then, invariably, life shows me that ethnicity matters.

Bensonhurst, the working-class neighborhood where I was born and grew up and where my mother still lives, has acquired a certain notoriety after Spike Lee's *Jungle Fever* (1991) and the murder of Yusuf Hawkins, an African American, in 1989—the event that motivated the first essay in this collection. The neighborhood remains largely segregated, although the issue of race can no longer be ignored. Still, in most ways, Bensonhurst has not changed—it has preserved Italian American culture as if in amber. Year after year, decade after decade, Italian American children settle near their parents or new Italians come to begin the process of becoming American. The street life, shopping, rhythms of Bensonhurst remain similar to those of my youth, with one astonishing addition: Asian American shops and families, strong and multigenerational, uncanny replicas of the Italian Americans among whom they now live.

The street mentioned in my title, Ocean Parkway, divides Italian and Jewish neighborhoods in Brooklyn; it is also a corridor that leads to the tunnels and bridges that link the borough to Manhattan. In my youth, Ocean Parkway was a boundary for religious groups; today, it bristles with racial tensions. It remains a prime Brooklyn address—a typical residence for groups that will soon move to "the city" or the suburbs. For Brooklynites, Ocean Parkway is a powerful state of mind and a symbol of upward mobility. I see it as a stage set, an anticipation, a preparation for the bastions of elite American life. For me, upward mobility was a two-step process: first Jewish culture, then middle-class American. The precise stages differ for each ethnic group and each person, but assimilation always has a double movement: first the desire to be like others; then the realization that the likeness is never complete. To use a metaphor: I will always be crossing Ocean Parkway; I have crossed it; I will never cross it.

I CANNOT SPEAK FIRSTHAND about the Italian American experience of immigration. Both my parents were born in the United States, though my mother lived in Calabria between the ages of four and sixteen, on a small, poor farm where the animals shared the main room. Pigs were a mainstay of farm life and she describes tending the family pig each year until the annual slaughter and making of sausages. "I liked the pigs when I fed them," she says wryly, "and I liked the pigs all year round when I ate them." That's a long way from my experiences, and yet its tough-mindedness formed some of what she passed on to me. She describes, still angrily after all these years, how her older sister (who arrived back in the United

States first) ridiculed her long braids and taste in clothes; how, as the youngest child, she was expected to live in her sister's house as a family maid and babysitter, even though she also worked in a mattress factory. How she missed out on certain experiences, such as breast-feeding her children, because she was told these experiences were not "American" but strictly for "greaseballs," slang for newly arrived Italians.

These stories nourished me—but they are the stories of my parents' and grandparents' generation. What I tell here is different from the story of arrival. It is the story of assimilation— one that Italian Americans of my generation are uniquely prepared to tell, and that females need to tell most of all.

Being ethnic has given me sensitive antennae for feeling out of it or excluded; but so has being female, a category often denigrated by Italian Americans. I have a strong attraction to powerful (largely male), upper- and upper-middle-class American culture. I want to feel privileged and entitled. At the same time, I identify, I *like to identify,* with outsiders. Much of my recent work has been about "us/them" relations in American culture and about a hunger for "primitive" Others. All of these concerns structure this volume, whose theme is crossings: crossings between ethnic groups and social classes, being an outsider and an insider; crossings between the roles of wife, mother, daughter, mourner, professional woman, critic, and writer. Part One is written in an intensive "I" voice and is largely about being Italian American and female; its essays are in the genre of memoir. Part Two uses my experiences to show how contradictory desires for community and individuality pervade icons of culture from Dr. Dolittle to Lionel Trilling, *The Godfather* to Camille Paglia. Its essays are cultural criticism and probe conflicts between ideas of moving up and a place of origin, acquisitiveness and integrity, male and female identity, the individual "I" and the cultural "We." But a central contention of this book is the crossing between personal history and intellectual life. So that the autobiographical essays are also about American society and autobiography erupts more and more into the readings of U.S. culture.

These essays record feelings of ambition and desire; nostalgia and disdain; fear and loss; coping and letting go; being a child, a parent, and the child of aging parents. In both the autobiographical and analytic mode, it's the human things these essays are after.

Note on the Text:

In the individual essays, I have retained time indicators appropriate to when each essay was originally written and have not attempted to bring ages, dates, and other facts in line with the year of book publication.

In the essays that are memoirs, some names and circumstances have been altered slightly.

PART ONE

Crossing Ocean Parkway

One

On Being White, Female, and Born in Bensonhurst

The Mafia protects the neighborhood, our fathers say, with that peculiar satisfied pride with which law-abiding Italian Americans refer to the Mafia: the Mafia protects "the neighborhood" from "the coloreds." In the fifties and sixties, I heard that information repeated, in whispers, in neighborhood parks and in the yard at school in Bensonhurst. The same information probably passes today in the parks (the word now "blacks," not "coloreds") but perhaps no longer in the school yards. From buses each morning, from neighborhoods outside Bensonhurst, spill children of all colors and backgrounds—American black, West Indian black, Hispanic, and Asian. But the blacks are the ones especially marked for notice. Bensonhurst is no longer entirely protected from "the coloreds." But in a deeper sense, at least for Italian Americans, Bensonhurst never changes.

Italian American life continues pretty much as I remember it. Families with young children live side by side with older couples whose children are long gone to the suburbs. Many of

those families live "down the block" from the previous generation or, sometimes still, live together with parents or grandparents. When a young family leaves, as sometimes happens,
for Long Island or New Jersey or (very common now) Staten
Island, another arrives, without any special effort being
required, from Italy or from a poorer neighborhood in New
York. They fill the neat but anonymous houses along the
mostly tree-lined streets: two-, three-, or four-family houses
for the most part (this is a working-class area, and people need
rents to pay mortgages), with a few single-family or small
apartment houses tossed in at random. Tomato plants, fig
trees, and plaster madonnas often decorate small but well-
tended yards that face out onto the street; the grassy front
lawn, like the grassy backyard, are relatively uncommon.

Crisscrossing the neighborhood and marking out ethnic
zones—Italian, Irish, and Jewish, for the most part, though
there are some Asian Americans and some people (usually
Protestants) called simply Americans—are the great shopping
streets: 86th Street, Kings Highway, Bay Parkway, 20th
Avenue, 18th Avenue, each with its own distinctive character.
On 86th Street, crowds bustle along sidewalks lined with
ample vegetable and fruit stands. Women wheeling shopping
carts or baby strollers check the fruit carefully, piece by piece,
and bargain with the dealer, cajoling for a better price or letting him know that the vegetables, this time, aren't up to snuff.
A few blocks down, the fruit stands are gone and the streets
are lined by clothing and record shops, mobbed by teen-agers.
Occasionally, the elevated train ("the El") rumbles overhead,
a few stops out of Coney Island on its way to "the city," a trip
of around one hour.

On summer nights, neighbors congregate on "stoops" that
during the day serve as play yards for children. Air-condition-
ing exists everywhere in Bensonhurst, but people still sit outside in the summer—to supervise children, to gossip, to stare

at strangers. "Buona sera," I say, or "Buona notte," as I am ritually presented to Sal and Lily and Louie: the neighbors, sitting on the stoop. "Grazie," I say when they praise my children or my appearance. It's the only time I use Italian, which I learned at high school, although my parents (both first-generation Italian Americans, my father Sicilian, my mother Calabrian) speak it at home, to each other, but never to me or my brother. My accent is the Tuscan accent taught at school, not the southern Italian accents of my parents and the neighbors.

It's important to greet and please the neighbors; any break in this decorum would seriously offend and aggrieve my parents. For the neighbors are second only to family in Bensonhurst and serve as stern arbiters of conduct. Does Lucy keep a clean house? Did Anna wear black long enough after her mother's death? Was the food good at Tony's wedding? The neighbors know and pass judgment. Any news of family scandal (my brother's divorces, for example) provokes from my mother the agonized words: "But what will I tell *people*?" I sometimes collaborate in devising a plausible script.

A large sign on the church I attended as a child for me sums up the ethos of neighborhoods like Bensonhurst. The sign urges contributions to the church building fund with the message, in huge letters: "EACH YEAR THIS CHURCH SAVES THIS NEIGHBORHOOD ONE MILLION DOLLARS IN TAXES." Passing the church on the way from largely Jewish and middle-class Sheepshead Bay (where my husband grew up) to Bensonhurst, year after year, my husband and I look for the sign and laugh at the crass level of its pitch, its utter lack of attention to things spiritual. But we also understand *exactly* the values it represents.

IN THE SUMMER OF 1989, my parents were visiting me at my house in Durham, North Carolina, from the apartment in Bensonhurst where they had lived since 1942, ever since the

day they had wed: three small rooms, rent-controlled, floor
clean enough to eat off, every corner and crevice known and
organized. My parents' longevity in a single apartment is
unusual even for Bensonhurst, but not that unusual; many
people live for decades in the same place or move within a ten-
block radius. When I lived in this apartment, there were four
rooms; one has since been ceded to a demanding "landlord,"
one of the various "landlords" who have haunted my parents'
life and must always be appeased lest the ultimate threat—
removal from the rent-controlled apartment—be brought into
play. That summer, during the time of their visit, on August
23rd (my younger daughter's birthday) a shocking, disturbing, news report issued from "the neighborhood": it had
become another Howard Beach.

Three black men, walking casually through the streets at
night, were attacked by a much larger group of whites. One
was shot dead, mistaken, as it turned out, for another black
youth who was dating a white, although part-Hispanic, girl in
the neighborhood. It all made sense: the crudely protective
men, expecting to see a black arriving at the girl's house and
overreacting; the rebellious girl dating the outsider boy; the
black dead as a sacrifice to the feelings of "the neighborhood."

I might have felt outrage, I might have felt guilt or shame,
I might have despised the people among whom I grew up: in
a way I felt all four emotions when I heard the news. I expect
that there were many people in Bensonhurst itself who felt the
same rush of emotions. But mostly I felt that, given the setup,
this was the only way things could have happened. I detested
the racial killing; but I also understood it. Those streets, which
should be public property, belong to "the neighborhood." All
the people sitting on the stoops on August 23rd knew that as
well as they knew their own names. The black men walking
through probably knew it too—though their casual walk
sought to deny the fact that, for the neighbors, even the sim-

ple act of blacks walking through "the neighborhood" would be seen as invasion.

Italian Americans in Bensonhurst are notable for their cohesiveness and provinciality; the slightest pressure turns those qualities into prejudice and racism. Their cohesiveness is based on the stable economic and ethical level that links generation to generation, keeping Italian Americans in Bensonhurst and the Italian American community alive as the Jewish American community of my youth is no longer alive. (Its young people routinely moved to the suburbs or beyond, and were never replaced, so that Jews in Bensonhurst today are almost all very old people.) Their provinciality results from the Italian Americans' devotion to jealous distinctions and discriminations. Jews are suspect but (the old Italian women admit) "they make good husbands." The Irish are okay, fellow Catholics, but not really "like us"; they make bad husbands because they drink and gamble. Even Italians come in varieties by region (Sicilian, Calabrian, Neapolitan, very rarely any region further north), and by history in this country (the newly arrived and ridiculed "gaffoon" versus the first or second generation).

Bensonhurst is a neighborhood dedicated to believing that its values are the only values; it tends towards certain forms of inertia. When my parents visit me in Durham, they routinely take chairs from the kitchen and sit out on the lawn in front of the house, not on the chairs on the back deck; then they complain that the streets are too quiet. When they walk around my neighborhood and look at the mailboxes they report (these De Marcos descended from Cozzitortos, who have friends named Travaglianti and Pelliccioni) that my neighbors have strange names. Prices at my local supermarket are compared, in unbelievable detail, with prices on 86th Street. Any rearrangement of my kitchen since their last visit is registered and criticized. Difference is not only unwelcome, it is unacceptable. One of the most characteristic things my mother ever said was in response to my plans for renovating my house in Durham. When she heard my plans, she looked around, crossed her arms, and said, "If it was me, I wouldn't change nothing." My father once asked me to level with him about a Jewish boyfriend, who lived in a different portion of the neighborhood, reacting to his Jewishness, but even more to the fact that he often wore Bermuda shorts: "Tell me something, Marianna. Is he a Communist?" Such are the standards of normalcy and political thinking in Bensonhurst.

I often think that one important difference between Italian Americans in neighborhoods like Bensonhurst and Italian Americans elsewhere is that the others moved on—to upstate New York, to Pennsylvania, to the Midwest. Though they often settled in communities of fellow Italians, they moved on. Bensonhurst Italian Americans seem to have felt that one large move, over the ocean, was enough. Future moves could only be local: from the Lower East Side, say, to Brooklyn, or from one part of Brooklyn to another. Bensonhurst was for many of these people the *summa* of expectations. If their America were to be drawn as a *New Yorker* cover, Manhattan would be tiny in proportion to Bensonhurst itself, and to its satellites, Staten Island, New Jersey, and Long Island.

"Oh, no," my father says when he hears the news about the shooting. Though he still refers to blacks as "coloreds," he's not really a racist and is upset that this innocent youth was shot in his neighborhood. He has no trouble acknowledging the wrongness of the death. But then, like all the news accounts, he turns to the fact, repeated over and over, that the blacks had been on their way to look at a used car when they encountered the hostile mob of whites. The explanation is right before him but, "Yeah," he says, still shaking his head, "yeah, but what were they *doing* there. They didn't belong." The "they," it goes without saying, refers to the blacks.

[As I write this essay, I am teaching Robert Frost: "What had that flower to do with being white / The wayside blue and innocent heal-all? / What brought the kindred spider to that height, / Then steered the white moth thither in the night? / What but design of darkness to appall?— / If design govern in a thing so small." Thus Frost in "Design" on a senseless killing and the ambiguity of causation and color symbolism. My father: "They didn't belong."]

OVER THE NEXT FEW DAYS, the TV news is even more disturbing. Rows of screaming Italians, lining the streets, many of them looking like my relatives. The young men wear undershirts and crosses dangle from their necks as they hurl curses. I focus especially on one woman who resembles almost completely my mother: stocky but not fat, mid-seventies but well preserved, full face showing only minimal wrinkles, ample steel-gray hair neatly if rigidly coiffed in a modified beehive hairdo left over from the sixties. She shakes her fist at the camera, protesting the arrest of the Italian American youths in the neighborhood and the incursion of more blacks into Bensonhurst, protesting the shooting. I look a little nervously at my mother (the parent I resemble) but she has not even noticed the woman and stares impassively at the television.

WHAT HAS BENSONHURST TO DO with what I teach today and write? Why did I need to write about this killing in Bensonhurst, but not in the manner of a news account or a statistical sociological analysis? Within days of hearing the news, I began to plan this essay, to tell the world what I knew, though I stopped midway, worried that my parents or their neighbors would hear about it. I sometimes think that I looked around from my baby carriage and decided that someday, the sooner the better, I would get out of Bensonhurst. Now, much to my surprise, Bensonhurst—the antipodes of the intellectual life I sought, the least interesting of places—had become a respectable intellectual topic. People would be willing to hear about Bensonhurst—and all by the dubious virtue of a racial killing in the streets.

The story as I would have to tell it would be to some extent a class narrative: about the difference between working class and upper middle class, dependence and a profession, Bensonhurst and a posh suburb. But I need to make it clear that I do not imagine myself as writing from a position of enormous self-satisfaction, or even enormous distance. You can take the girl out of Bensonhurst (that much is clear); but you may not be able to take Bensonhurst out of the girl. Upward mobility is not the essence of the story, though it is an important marker and symbol.

In Durham today, I live in a modern house, surrounded by an acre of trees. When I sit on my back deck, on summer evenings, no houses are visible through the trees. I have a guaranteed income, teaching English at an excellent university, removed by my years of education from the fundamental economic and social conditions of Bensonhurst. The one time my mother ever expressed pleasure at my work was when I got tenure—what my father called, with no irony intended, "ten years." "What does that mean?" my mother said when she heard the news. Then she reached back into her experiences as a garment worker, subject to seasonal "layoffs": "Does it mean they can't fire you just for nothing and can't lay you off?" When I said that was exactly what it means, she said, "Very good. Congratulations. *That's wonderful.*" I was free from the bosses and from the network of petty anxieties that had formed, in large part, her very existence. Of course, I wasn't really free of petty anxieties: would my salary increase keep pace with my colleagues', how would my office compare, would this essay be accepted for publication, am I happy? The line between these worries and my mother's is the line between the working class and the upper middle class.

But getting out of Bensonhurst never meant to me a big house, or nice clothes, or a large income. And it never meant feeling good about looking down on what I left behind or hiding my background. Getting out of Bensonhurst meant freedom—to experiment, to grow, to change. It also meant knowledge in some grand, abstract way. All the material possessions I have acquired, I acquired simply along the way—and for the first twelve years after I left Bensonhurst, I chose to acquire almost nothing at all. Now, as I write about "the neighborhood," I recognize that although I've come far in physical and material distance, the emotional distance is harder to gauge. Bensonhurst has everything to do with who I am and even with what I write. "We can never cease to be ourselves" (Conrad, *The Secret Agent*). Occasionally I get reminded of my roots, of their simultaneously choking and nutritive power.

Scene One: It's after a lecture at Duke, given by a visiting professor of German from a major university. The lecture was long and I'm tired but—bad luck—I had agreed to be one of the people having dinner with the lecturer afterwards. I settle into the table at the restaurant with my companions: this man, the head of the Comparative Literature program (also a professor of German), and a couple I like who teach French. The conversation is sluggish, as it often is when a stranger, in this case the visiting professor, has to be assimilated into a group. So I ask the visitor a question to personalize things: "How did you get interested in what you do? What made you become a professor of German?" The man gets going and begins talking about how it was really unlikely that he, a nice Jewish boy from Bensonhurst, would have chosen, in the mid-fifties, to study German. Unlikely indeed.

I remember seeing *Judgment at Nuremberg* in a local movie theater and having a woman in the row in back of me get hysterical when some clips of a concentration camp were shown; "My God," she screamed in a European accent, "look at what they did. Murderers, MURDERERS!"—and she had to be supported out by her family. I couldn't see, in the dark, whether her arm bore the neatly tattooed numbers that the arms of some of my classmates' parents did—and that always affected me with a thrill of horror. This man is about ten years older than I am; he had lived more directly through those feelings, lived every day at home with those feelings. The first chance he got he raced to study German. I myself have twice chosen not to visit Germany—but I would understand an impulse to identify with the Other as a way of getting out of the neighborhood.

At the dinner, the memory about the movie pops into my mind but I pick up instead on Bensonhurst—I'm also from there, but Italian American. Like a flash, he asks something I haven't been asked in years: Where did I go to high school and (a more common question) what was my family name? I went to Lafayette High School, I say, and my name was De Marco. Everything changes: his facial expression, his posture, his accent, his voice. "Soo Dee Maw-ko," he sez, "dun anything wrong at school today—got enny pink slips? Wanna meet me later at the park or maybe bye the Baye?" When I laugh, recognizing the stereotype that Italians get pink slips for misconduct at school and the notorious chemistry between Italian women and Jewish men, he says, back in his elegant voice: "My God, for a minute I felt like I was turning into a werewolf."

It's odd that although I can remember almost nothing else about this man—his face, his body type, even his name—I remember this lapse into his "real self" with enormous vividness. I am especially struck by how easily he was able to slip into the old, generic Brooklyn accent. I myself have no memory of ever speaking in that accent, though I also have no memory of trying *not* to speak it, except for teaching myself, carefully, to say "oil" rather than "earl."

But the surprises aren't over. The female French professor,

whom I have known for at least five years, reveals for the first time that she is also from "the neighborhood," though she lived on the other side of Kings Highway, went to a different, more elite high school, and is Irish American. Three of six professors, sitting at an "eclectic" vegetarian restaurant in Durham, all from Bensonhurst—a neighborhood where (I swear) you couldn't get the *New York Times* at any of the local stores.

Scene Two: In this scene, I still live in Bensonhurst. I'm waiting for my parents to return from a conference at my school, where they've been summoned to discuss my transition from elementary to junior high school. I am already a full year younger than any of my classmates, having been "skipped" a grade, a not uncommon occurrence for "gifted" youngsters. Now the school is worried about putting me in an accelerated track through junior high, since that would make me two years younger. A compromise is reached: I will be put in a special program for "gifted" children, but one that takes three, not two years. It sounds okay.

Three years later, another wait. My parents have gone to school to make another decision. Lafayette High School has three tracks: academic, for potentially college-bound kids; secretarial, mostly for Italian American girls or girls with low aptitude scores; and vocational, mostly for boys with the same attributes, ethnic or intellectual. (The high school is segregated de facto so none of the tracks is as yet racially coded, though they are coded by ethnic group and gender.) Although my scores are superb, the guidance counselor has recommended the secretarial track; when I protested, the conference with my parents was arranged. My mother's preference is clear: the secretarial track—college is for boys; I will need to make a "good living" until I marry and have children. My father also prefers the secretarial track, but he wavers, half proud of my aberrantly high scores, half worried. I press the attack, saying that if I were Jewish I would have been placed, without question, in the academic track. I tell him I have sneaked a peek at my files and know that my IQ is genius level. I am allowed to insist on the change into the academic track.

What I had done, and I was ashamed of it even then, was to play upon my father's competitive feelings with Jews: his daughter could and should be as good as theirs. In the bank where he was a messenger and the insurance company where he worked in the mail room, my father worked with Jews, who were almost always his immediate supervisors. Several times, my father was offered the supervisory job but turned it down, after long conversations with my mother about the dangers of making a change, the difficulty of giving orders to friends. After her work sewing dresses in a local garment shop, after cooking dinner and washing the floor each night, my mother often did "piecework" making bows for a certain amount of money per bow; sometimes I would help her for fun, but it *wasn't* fun and I was free to stop while she continued for long, tedious hours to increase the family income. Once a week, her part-time boss, Dave, would come by to pick up the boxes of bows. Short, round, with his shirttails sloppily tucked into his pants and a cigar almost always dangling from his lips, Dave was a stereotypical Jew but also, my parents always said, a nice guy, a decent man. The first landlord I remember was Mrs. Rosenberg. My father was a sitting duck.

Years later, similar choices come up and I show the same assertiveness I showed with my father, the same ability to deal for survival, but tinged with Bensonhurst caution. Where will I go to college? Not to Brooklyn College, the flagship of the city system—I know that, but don't press the invitations I have received to apply to prestigious schools outside of New York City. The choice comes down to two: Barnard, which gives me a full scholarship, minus five hundred dollars a year that all scholarship students are expected to contribute from summer earnings, or New York University, which offers me a thousand dollars above tuition. I waver. My parents stand firm: they are already losing money by letting me go to college; I owe it to the family to contribute the extra thousand plus my summer earnings. Besides, my mother adds, harping on a favorite theme, there are no boys at Barnard; at N.Y.U. I'm more likely to meet someone to marry. I go to N.Y.U., and marry in my senior year, but someone I didn't meet at college. I am secretly relieved, I think now (though at the time I thought I was just placating my parents' conventionality), to be out of the marriage sweepstakes.

The first boy who ever asked me for a date was Robert Zuckerman, in eighth grade: tall and skinny to my average height and pre-teen chubbiness. I turned him down, thinking we would make a ridiculous couple. Day after day, I cast my eyes at stylish Juliano, the class cutup; day after day, I captivated Robert Zuckerman. Occasionally, one of my brother's Italian American friends would ask me out, and I would go, often to R.O.T.C. dances; my specialty was making political remarks so shocking that the guys rarely asked again. After a while, I recognized destiny: the Jewish man was a passport out of Bensonhurst. When I married, I of course did marry a Jewish man, who gave me my freedom, and, very important, helped remove me from the expectations of Bensonhurst. Though raised in a largely Jewish section of Brooklyn, he had gone to college in Ohio and knew how important it was (as he put it) "to get past the Brooklyn Bridge"; we met on neutral ground, in Central Park, at a performance of Shakespeare. The Jewish-Italian marriage is a common enough catastrophe in Bensonhurst for my parents to have accepted, even welcomed my marriage—though my parents continued to treat my husband as an outsider for the first twenty years ("Now Mary Ann. Here's what's going on with you' brother. But don't tell you' husband").

Along the way, I make other choices, more fully marked by Bensonhurst cautiousness. I am attracted to journalism or the arts as careers, but the prospects for income seem iffy. I choose instead to imagine myself as a teacher. Only the availability of NDEA Fellowships when I graduate, with their generous terms, propels me from high school teaching (a thought I never much relished) to college teaching (which seems like a brave new world). Within college teaching, I choose offbeat specializations: the novel, interdisciplinary approaches (not something clear and clubby, like Milton or the eighteenth century). Eventually I write the book I like best about "primitive" Others as they figure within Western obsessions: my identification with "the Other," my sense of being "Other," surfaces at last. I avoid all mentoring structures for a long time, but accept aid when it comes to me on the basis of what I perceive to be merit. I'm still, deep down, Italian American Bensonhurst, though by this time I'm a lot of other things as well.

Scene Three: In the summer of 1988, a little more than a year before the shooting in Bensonhurst, my father woke up trembling and in what appeared to be a fit. Hospitalization revealed that he had a pocket of blood on his brain, a frequent consequence of falls for older people. About a year earlier, I had stayed home, heeding my father's suggestion that I remain with my children, when my aunt, my father's much-loved sister, died; only now does my mother tell me how much my father resented my missing the funeral. Now, confronted with what is described as "brain surgery," but turns out to be less dramatic than it sounds, I fly to New York immediately.

My brother drives three hours back and forth from New Jersey every day to drive my mother and me to the hospital, which is about fifteen minutes from my parents' apartment: he is being a fine Italian American son. Often, for the first time in years, we have long conversations alone. He is two years older than I am, a chemical engineer who has also left "the neighborhood," but has remained closer to its values, with a suburban, Republican inflection. He talks a lot about New York, saying that (except for neighborhoods like Bensonhurst) it's a "Third World city now." It's the summer of the Tawana Brawley incident, when Brawley accused white men of abducting her and smearing racial slurs on her body with her own excrement. My brother is filled with dislike for Al Sharpton and Brawley's other vocal supporters in the black community—not because they are black but because they are "troublemakers, stirring things up." The city is drenched in racial hatred that makes itself felt in the halls of the hospital: Italians and Jews in the beds and as doctors; blacks as nurses and orderlies.

This is the first time since I left New York in 1975 that I have visited Brooklyn without once getting into Manhattan. It's the first time I have spent several days alone with my mother, living in her apartment in Bensonhurst. My every move is scrutinized and commented on. I feel like I am going to go crazy.

Finally, it's clear that my father is going to be fine and I can go home. My mother insists on accompanying me to the travel agent to get my ticket home, even though I really want to be alone. The agency (a Mafia front?) has no one who knows how to ticket me for the exotic destination of North Carolina and no computer for doing so. The one person who can perform this feat by hand is out. I have to kill time for an hour and suggest to my mother that she go home, to be there for my brother when he arrives from Jersey. We stop in a Pork Store, where I buy a stash of cheeses, sausages, and other delicacies unavailable in Durham. My mother walks home with the shopping bags, and I'm on my own.

More than anything I want a kind of sorbetto or "ice" I remember from growing up called a "cremolata": almond-vanilla flavored, with large chunks of nuts. I pop into the local bakery (at an unlikely 11 A.M.) and ask for a cremolata, usually eaten after dinner. The woman—a younger version of my mother—refuses: they haven't made a fresh ice yet and what's left from the day before is too icy, no good. I explain that I'm about to get on a plane for North Carolina and want that ice, no good or not. But she has her standards and holds her ground, even though North Carolina has about the same status in her mind as Timbuktu and she knows I will be banished, perhaps forever, from the land of cremolata.

Then, while I'm taking a walk, enjoying my solitude, I have another idea. Near my parents' house, there's a club for men from a particular town or region in Italy: six or seven tables, some on the sidewalk beneath a garish red, green, and white sign; no women allowed or welcome unless they're with the men; and no women at all during the day when the real business of the club—a game of cards for old men who would be much quainter in Italy than they are in Bensonhurst—is in progress. Still, I know that inside the club would be coffee and a cremolata ice. I'm thirty-eight, well dressed, very respectable looking; I know what I want. I also know I'm not supposed to enter that club. I enter anyway, asking the teenage boy behind the counter firmly, in my most professorial tones, for a cremolata ice. Dazzled, he complies immediately. The old men at the card table have been staring at this scene, unable to place me, exactly, though my facial type is familiar. Finally, a few old men's hisses pierce the air. "Strega," I hear as I leave, "mala strega," "witch," or "brazen whore." I have been in Bensonhurst less than a week but I have managed to reproduce, on my final day there for this visit, the conditions of my youth. Knowing the rules, I have broken them. I shake hands with my discreetly rebellious past, still an outsider walking through the neighborhood, marked and insulted—though unlikely to be shot.

T w o

Crossing Ocean Parkway

I

Summer 1991. Crown Heights. Another racial killing. This time it began with an accident. A Hasidic man lost control of his car, jumped the curb, and hit two black children, killing seven-year-old Gavin Cato. A private ambulance operated by the Lubavitcher Jewish community arrived to treat the driver. Some of the blacks in the neighborhood erupted in rage. Three hours later, a young rabbinical student from Australia named Yankel Rosenbaum was walking along the streets, oblivious to what had happened a few blocks away. He was attacked by a mob and stabbed four times, dying later in the hospital. The city was filled with a frenzy of hate. Al Sharpton and his supporters took to the streets; so did some Jewish groups in Crown Heights. It was a repetition of the murder of Yusuf Hawkins and its aftermath in Bensonhurst.[1]

This incident did not take place in my neighborhood. Crown Heights is on the other side of Brooklyn and is organized around Eastern Parkway, sister boulevard to Ocean Parkway, the street that orients my part of Brooklyn. Crown

19

Heights has long been a Jewish neighborhood, shared uneasily in recent decades with African and Caribbean Americans. But although it was across town and years away from my life in Brooklyn, this incident still touched a place I considered home.

THE TRAGEDY OF MY PARENTS' lives was that they never bought a house. It was a tragedy I came to feel too: the desire for more space, for places to putter, for a yard, for security beyond a landlord's fickle goodwill. Week after week, my family would travel to Rockaway, Flatlands, Staten Island before the Verrazano Bridge, to look at houses. We would assign bedrooms in our minds; we would make calculations. Sometimes, my parents even drew up contracts; I always hoped they would sign, but they never did. Always my parents begged off, afraid of not being able to meet the payments. We continued to live in a tiny apartment in Bensonhurst and to envy the houses and larger apartments along streets like Ocean Parkway.

When I married, it was to a Jewish man who had grown up on the other, Jewish, side of Ocean Parkway—though he had left Brooklyn (very deliberately) when he went to college. His parents owned a house in Sheepshead Bay—a two-family house in which they occupied the top floor. Loving people, they accepted me uncritically into their family circle. When I still lived in Bensonhurst, the four rooms on this top floor seemed very large and the house seemed like a symbol of middle-class life. There it was, solid brick, accumulating value, representing the security in old age that made my parents so anxious. It was a place my husband and I made love, a place where our babies' pictures took pride of place on every wall. Even after it ceased to seem grand, that house was our outpost in New York—where we would stay when we visited the city from New England or, later on, North Carolina. From this house, we could buy knishes or pastrami, drink egg creams at the local candy store, sample the rest of Brooklyn's Jewish life.

The rhythm of my life in this house came to an end when my father-in-law died late in July 1991. My mother-in-law was unable to live alone, so we moved her to Florida to live with her grandson and his family, arranging for her house to be emptied and painted. One night, about a week after the Crown Heights incident, I got a call from my sister-in-law, who lives in the same part of Florida. Her voice was shaking and I was afraid something had happened to my mother-in-law. But it wasn't her, it was the house. Someone had broken in to the empty top floor and sprayed the newly painted walls with anti-Semitic signs and slogans. Where the daily *Forward* once sat, there were slurs about Jews and money and Israel. The mirrored wall in the living room reflected back the looker's image through large red swastikas.

There were different theories about who did it: some African American kids from the housing projects across Nostrand Avenue, incited by the Crown Heights incident? That was the leading theory, but there were others: some Italian kids pissed off that my father-in-law hadn't paid them in full for a paint job they didn't do well? a disgruntled boyfriend of the tenant downstairs who used his key to enter the apartment? somebody with no special motive at all? Whoever did it, it was an outrage and a desecration, an insult to my in-laws that we cannot even be sure was aimed at them in any purposeful way. In the life of the city, it was a minor incident, worthy of a police report but not of further investigation.

The event took me back to Brooklyn, not literally this time but still in a powerful way, in my feelings and my mind. I was thinking about that house—what it symbolized in 1991 (one of my last ties to Brooklyn, a worry, a potential inheritance) and what it symbolized when I was still a teenager in Bensonhurst. Back then, the house symbolized the other side of Ocean

Parkway. And Ocean Parkway symbolized something different from the Italian American community of my youth. It symbolized upward mobility, which, as an Italian American girl in Brooklyn, I associated with Jews—the only available models. When I was growing up, it seemed as if Jews had the talent, ambition, and drive. Ergo, Jews and upward mobility went together in my mind.

I was doing the kind of ethnic thinking that is all too typical of New York, where groups live side by side but often have little intimate contact. In Crown Heights, ethnic thinking fueled the murder and the rage: the Jews have it all—all the money, all the power—We've got to stick together, like they do; or, from the Lubavitcher Jews, We've got to learn from the blacks and riot to get what we want. My relationship to Jews was a gentler form of ethnic thinking that for me opened up possibilities. I believed in an idealized, almost imaginary version of what it meant to be Jewish—for which I feel the kind of nostalgia one can feel only for adopted cultures or for those that no longer exist.

II

Ocean Parkway is a monument to the grand urban planning of the nineteenth century, which took an unexpected turn in the twentieth. The street uncoils from Frederick Law Olmsted's elegant Prospect Park, with its pathways for bikes and horses, lake with boathouse, and mown fields, and functions as both highway and continuation of the Park. As with Eastern Parkway, which he also designed, Olmsted meant for it to be the proud center of a proud Brooklyn—Brooklyn when it was a cultural magnet and not just a bedroom for Manhattan.[2] Eastern Parkway was Brooklyn's cultural jewel—housing its museum, botanical gardens, and public library and running from Prospect Park into Queens; Ocean Parkway was its residential jewel, running from Prospect Park to the Atlantic Ocean. Broad and multi-laned, Ocean Parkway stretches across the borough, funneling traffic to and from Manhattan or downtown Brooklyn and the sandy plains of Coney Island. It is lined by rows of trees and wide, leaf-bedappled, concrete paths divided neatly down the middle by benches for pedestrians or bikers taking a rest. Along the sidewalks are closely massed but elegant apartment houses or grand one-family houses, often in a vaguely Spanish, tile-roofed style. The impression I am trying to convey is of ease and spaciousness in the middle of a crowded borough. Ease and spaciousness are the essence of Ocean Parkway and the reason why, for Brooklynites, Ocean Parkway is a powerful state of mind.

Even today, any day of the week, but especially on weekends, Ocean Parkway is a destination for pedestrians for miles around. Bikers ride up and down beneath the trees and then off onto the bike paths of Prospect Park. Occasionally, riders on horseback prance down the paths. Old people sit on the benches for long hours, reading newspapers or gossiping with friends. Teenagers stroll by in their finery, with couples lingering on the benches. Around the turn of the century, there would have been a similar scene but with a different cast of characters. I imagine ladies with parasols, gents with hats, and motorcars moving slowly down the Parkway to the beautiful, wide beaches at its southern end. The ethnic identity of the people with the parasols and hats, the people in the motorcars, is vague in my imagination; they are what Brooklynites today call "Americans," the rough equivalent of white, Anglo-Saxon, and Protestant.

When I was young, in the fifties and sixties, the "Americans" were already gone or huddled in the protective enclaves of Brooklyn Heights and Park Slope. Brooklyn was just a borough, a satellite to sparkling Manhattan, a place where famous writers used to live. Families of Jews—reform and Orthodox, Ashkenazi and Sephardic—walked along the pathways of

Ocean Parkway to or from *shul.* Women with kerchief-covered heads wheeled baby strollers and corralled an incredible number of young children; their husbands, some wearing hats and *pais,* sidecurls, walked nearby, in groups of men. On Sundays, the Jews wore ordinary dress and the Catholics donned their finery.

On its far northern end, near Prospect Park, the last ten years have added new elements to the Jewish-Catholic mix typical of Ocean Parkway in my youth. African Americans, Caribbean Americans, Hispanics, and a growing population of Asians now occupy housing near the Parkway and stroll its corridors too. The street shows signs of uneasy resistance. Apartment buildings sport placards that announce their conversion into condominiums whose purchasers must pass the appropriate committees. The fortress architecture always typical of local synagogues is accentuated in the most recent ones. At around its midpoint from north to south, the population shifts. Black and Hispanic faces disappear; the Jewish and Italian faces I remember from my youth dominate once again. Even here there are changes: many of the Jews now are from Russia, and the signs over their shops are sometimes in the Cyrillic alphabet.

An ecumenical crossroads, the Jerusalem of Brooklyn, Ocean Parkway remains an important boundary for ethnic groups, and an important rite of passage. For me it was a training school, a dress rehearsal for the bastions of American culture.

III

The first apartments I entered on Ocean Parkway, around 1964, belonged to Jewish high-school classmates. In Joan Karp's apartment, we talked about college and writing, listened to Vivaldi, and read Keats (with, in Joan's phrase, "sympathy and sorrow"). In David Sultan's Orthodox Sephardic household, we dabbled in kisses, debated the ethics of romance, and pondered the sources of religious thinking. These were important entries, my first participation with real people in intellectual life. Like all my Jewish friends, Joan and David simply expected to go to college; my Italian friends mostly did not. Gradually, through the high school years, I shifted alliances.

I do not remember this as being, at the time, a painful process. I had convinced myself already that Italian Americans did not value girls and especially girls who were good at the kinds of things I liked—reading, thinking, and writing. In my private mythology, I was despised by my family as unfeminine and unseemly. That in retrospect this seems not to have been entirely true hardly matters—it was what literary critics call an enabling fiction. I had many fantasies about life outside of Bensonhurst, in "the city" and beyond, fantasies of the most "American" kind, about upward mobility in a feminine key.

Most of these fantasies came from television: wealthy Sky King and his niece Penny, ranchers in Texas with a private plane to fly into and out of adventures. I was Penny—amiable, blond, ponytailed sidekick. There was the all-male family in *Bonanza,* to which I added a sister, Little Joe's twin, Amanda—dark-haired this time, a role I fit better physically—where I spent a lot of time in daydreams. My aspirations were that specific yet that fanciful: a stalwart Texas twosome, a massive ranch in Nevada, private airplanes and horses—things all but unknown in Brooklyn. The closest I came to the real world was admiring Jackie Kennedy and thinking how great it would be to be First Lady (as a female, I was never so bold as to think: President).

Although my daydreams circled around Ur-WASPs like

Sky King and the Cartwrights, in Brooklyn I never encountered any and did not even know what the term WASP meant. But I did encounter Jews—as principals and teachers: people who would judge me and control my potential to continue onward. As classmates in the "advanced" courses," those who seemed destined for the best colleges, careers, and suburbs. And so I tagged along—one of the "smart" ones along with the Jewish kids—able to participate in their lives at school and gradually, through high school, outside of school as well. More of my friends were Jewish. Most of my dates were with Jewish men, whose mothers would sometimes interfere to break things up. But this was always gentle not hurtful stuff, since the relationships involved were never serious.

When I was a junior in college I entered the apartment that most fulfilled my association of Jews with "culture"—Dick Chernick's apartment near Ditmas Avenue with its balcony overlooking Ocean Parkway. Dick Chernick was a high school teacher who had taught my boyfriend (later my husband) history. When Dick and Stu, my husband, met by chance during Stu's college years, they became good friends; I entered the scene a year into that friendship. Tall and slim, Dick had careful, elegant hands, a wide smile that would burst suddenly on his face and an almost silent laugh that registered in wrinkles.

His Ocean Parkway apartment was, like his personality itself, an oasis of thought and tranquility. His apartment was always available for dinner, or a talk, or as a place to stay. There were always good books lying around, and journals like the *New York Review of Books,* which I first read there. The food was always effortless but delicious, with the freshest possible vegetables. Classical music or jazz were the norms but, in keeping with Dick's left-to-radical political sympathies, I first heard Paul Robeson there. Dick always had a pet or two—usually a sumptuously beautiful and well-behaved cat. Zen-like and cat-like himself, Dick Chernick always listened intently and was never in a great hurry to respond. Feelings would get expressed in his apartment and be allowed to hang there, for all of us to ponder and absorb, not necessarily to dissect. Politics were a routine part of the discussion too. The talk was passionate but not argumentative and no one used loud voices.

I loved Dick Chernick practically from the first moment I saw him—in the way that a student loves a teacher who becomes, against all the odds, a close friend. He represented a life I felt in my grasp now that I was finishing college and spending lots of time in "the city." I looked to him for approval and beamed inwardly when he picked up on my remarks or observations—a good girl, a good student, this has always been my biggest intellectual vice. When I argued with my parents—as I often did—Dick's place was available to blow off steam, gain some perspective, or just to be away from my family.

There were two other Ocean Parkway apartments of Jewish acquaintances that became important during these years, the late sixties. They belonged to what I call the "two Alans"— Alan F. and Alan N.[3] In September 1968, my future husband and these men were hired as teachers by the Community School Board in Ocean Hill–Brownsville during the famous strike over "community control" of the schools. The New York City Teachers' Union, which was largely Jewish, was on strike to protest community control; the Ocean Hill–Brownsville board, which was black, retaliated by hiring new young teachers like my husband. This famous strike ruptured relationships between blacks and Jews in New York, who had been perceived as allies earlier in the sixties, during the Civil Rights struggle. Its politics were unusual, since liberals like my husband, who would normally support strikes, broke the strike in order to support the principle of community control. The new teachers were drawn partly by the idealistic goal of teaching the "underprivileged" in an experimental system, and partly by the availability of teaching deferments from the draft during the Vietnam War.

Alan F. and his wife were a cheerful, hip-seeming couple we saw five or six times before discovering we had little in common outside of our husbands' work. They lived in a new, relatively high-rise building that was, to my way of thinking, peculiarly situated. On one side, it overlooked the busy but elegant street itself; on the other, it overlooked a graveyard. Apartments on the graveyard side were cheaper, and, according to Alan, if you chose the right window coverings, the view was okay and the neighbors were quiet. Alan and Naomi lived in what was called a "junior three." In the jargon of Ocean Parkway that meant that the dining room was part of the living room, rather than occupying the separate alcove that distinguished the senior three. At dinner in their apartment, Naomi jumped up repeatedly to thoroughly rinse the dishes after each course. The next course would be punctuated by the noisy rumble of the dishwasher from the adjoining kitchen. My feelings towards this apartment were distinctly mixed. Slickly decorated in nouveau contemporary style (it had been the building's model apartment), it inspired certain covetous feelings. But I hated the dishwasher's noise even as I wondered what it would be like to have one. And I wondered what it would be like to have a doorman who insisted on substantial monthly bribes called "tips," but was also suspected of orchestrating a rash of burglaries in the building. Ocean Parkway was becoming the symbol of something other than culture, spaciousness, and ease: it was acquiring a grasping, greedy, middle-class subtext.

The quintessential Ocean Parkway couple came to seem, however, not Alan F. and his wife but Alan N. and his wife, Elaine—music lovers, with whom we shared a few evenings listening to favorite opera records. Alan and Elaine were marking time, anxiously, before they could move to the suburbs. In the meantime, Ocean Parkway was the only place to be. Alan N. loved Ocean Parkway—to him it really *was* Jerusalem, to be exceeded only by some new Jerusalem, like Great Neck. He loved every inch of the Parkway, but especially the block between Avenues M and N where he lived, and especially his building, with its classical Italianate nymph fountain out front, bathed in colored lights. Dinner at this apartment featured much talk about night courses to get pay increments for teachers, junior fours on the horizon, which view in the building was to be preferred, and saving for houses. It also featured ritual displays of the silver Alan and Elaine had purchased before their wedding—a seashell pattern I can't identify by name but have seen a lot since. The pattern was in good taste; but it would be whisked away, back to its box, before we ever sat down to dinner.

In many ways, Alan N. and his wife wanted what I did in the late sixties: material things, a house in the suburbs, an incremental rise up the social ladder. I was now almost in a position to get them. But I didn't like seeing these kinds of goals reflected back to me in other people whose ideas seemed too personal and petty by far. The cud was turning sour even as I chewed it. More than that, it was the late sixties. Materialism was out, Left politics and hippie communalism were in. My new husband's friends tended to be political activists— against the Vietnam War, midwifing the Age of Aquarius. Some of the groups we attended were fairly radical; one ended when a man we knew only slightly blew himself up with the Greenwich Village brownstone where he was building bombs. I was one step behind in the scramble for political commitment and rejection of material things. But I found the lure of the counterculture as attractive as the siren call of upward mobility.

IV

Reenter Dick Chernick, for the second half of his story. In the late sixties, Dick voluntarily left largely white, middle-class Sheepshead Bay High School to teach at a poverty-racked black and Hispanic high school on the Lower East Side; he helped keep the school open, with an experimental curriculum, during the 1968 teachers' strike. Then he left Ocean Parkway first for downtown Brooklyn, then for the Lower East Side. A few years later, he left New York for a cozy shack surrounded by simple gardens in rural western New Jersey—a place so isolated that it's hard to recognize as New Jersey at all. He adopted a boisterous dog named Teezee whose owner had died. With the dog and cats, the abundant gardens, and the peacefulness of it all, Dick Chernick reminded me of Dr. Dolittle, a childhood hero. He went from straight to gay and back to straight, and (in the move from city to country) from high school teaching to being janitor in an old-age home, a job that, having given up on teaching, he loved for its simplicity.

All of these moves were absolutely and completely right for Dick Chernick. Every gesture, every meal, every vase and pot in his various households testified to the rightness of his way of life until, Gemini-like, he would be on to the next one. Other people could fall from grace; but for me Dick was one of the authentically graceful. Whether he was strolling near the Williamsburg bridge or weeding his gardens in New Jersey, Dick always seemed totally at one with his surroundings.

Dick sometimes told his life as a comedy of errors: joining the Navy after high school, his sexual identity always in flux—and what *was* his relationship to his father and several stepfathers, whom he rarely mentioned? Like mine, his history followed the trends of the times, the ethos of different decades. Yet he never seemed like a victim of mediated desire—wanting things because other people said you should. He seemed totally there and totally right, alert to all the possibilities of himself and the world around him. His secret was not, as I thought at first, having the material things or cultural capital I associated with Ocean Parkway, but seeing beyond them. His secret was being "there"—wherever you happened to be—with awareness and acceptance, without racing on to the next thing to be done, gotten, or spent. I recognized Dick's spirituality even as I also realized that, if I imitated him, I might never cross Ocean Parkway. So through the seventies and eighties, as Dick Chernick was casting things off, I was gradually taking them on.

The last time I saw Dick Chernick he was smiling broadly, dressed (uncharacteristically) in a suit, and holding a bouquet of flowers destined for the mother of the woman he was soon to marry. Marriage was to be the last of Dick's many changes that I knew about, a surprise even to himself. Dick got out of the car in which we had driven into Manhattan, and walked away, turning to wave his flowers jauntily. I remember him most vividly, however, from the years before this last meeting, sitting in a rocking chair knitting, a woolen cap pushed back on his much-receded hairline—a memory from a winter evening in his New Jersey home, but a habit he had continued from his years on Ocean Parkway.

After 1981, when I moved to North Carolina, it became difficult to see Dick. Still in tune with our generation, my husband and I had entered an era of getting and spending, without even realizing the differences that would make. We had a new house, two young children, and were caught up in the busyness of everyday life. My husband's new job, as a stockbroker at Merrill Lynch, made it difficult for him to take extra days to drive out into western New Jersey during our short trips to New York. I wasn't independent enough to go myself. As time passed, communication with Dick became reduced to postcards and Christmas cards with brief messages. But that didn't worry my husband or me, since Dick was the kind of friend with whom communication could always be reestablished; anyway, we didn't really have the time to think about it.

After 1985, Dick's cards stopped coming and sometimes though not always my cards would be returned, marked "addressee unknown"—the vagaries, I thought, of a rural post office. In 1987, I received back my card with the intermittent "addressee unknown" stamp. But carrier #25 had taken the time this year to scrawl, cryptically, "deceased."

The word pierced the fog of my husband's busyness, and of my own absorption in work and children. We called the mail carrier (who was almost, but not quite sure Dick had died) and then tried to contact the many people we had known through Dick. We had been mobile during these years and they had too: lead after lead (mother, brother, lovers, friends) were missing from their last addresses and phone numbers, and they were untraceable. It was a parable of our culture's mobility.

Finally, in 1989, my husband played his trump card, tracing a man with an unmistakable name who had lived with Dick on the Lower East Side and for a while in New Jersey. He told us Dick had died, at least four years earlier, of a heart attack, at the old-age home where he worked. The man had wanted to attend the funeral but didn't, debilitated by the recent deaths of too many different friends from AIDS. He was not at all surprised to hear from Stu after an interval of perhaps ten years, nor was he reluctant to share Stu's belated grief; somehow, no one who had really known Dick Chernick would be. That night, my husband and I sat for the whole night crying and reminiscing. It was for us an epochal death, a marker of time's nasty tendency to slip away unnoticed, a measure of space traveled and roads perhaps unwisely taken. It was a return to the past that also marked an irrevocable break. Life spinning out of control while your eyes are on the wrong prize. People and places taken for granted—then suddenly gone forever.

V

My mother-in-law has now been uprooted from her house near Ocean Parkway. Outside of her own house, her decline is more visible. The mysteries of hallways confuse her; she has to be guided back and forth to her room. She asks the same questions over and over; we give the same answers, ignoring the repetition but pained by it. Now we understand the black smears that had appeared along the walls of the house in Sheepshead Bay: she holds the walls as she walks. We suspect that one reason my father-in-law did not want to leave Brooklyn was to hide her decline from what we learn is Alzheimer's disease. Clearly, we tell ourselves, she could not have lived alone; we were right to move her out of Brooklyn.

Yet in Florida she exists isolated, in a culture apart. People can't understand her culture and ways, so different from their own. My mother-in-law complains all the time—who's too fat or too thin, what we could have had for dinner instead of what we're having, and so on; she looks wounded when any request, however trivial, is denied, but she continues to make requests until she gets a denial. I try to explain to my niece, a native Floridian, for a while her main caretaker, that the complaining is cultural, normal, my mother-in-law's form of communication, not to be taken all that seriously. But I take it seriously myself, identifying with her more than I ever have, now that she is away from home and out of culture.

Looking for clues, I read Barbara Myerhoff's account of a Jewish center in California, *Number Our Days*, which claims that the connection to *Yiddishkeit*, Yiddish culture, is crucial for the old people about whom she wrote. I decide that my mother-in-law would do better if we could put her back in touch with her culture. The next time I try to talk to my mother-in-law on the phone, I ask whether anyone at her Jewish center speaks Yiddish and whether she might like us to find one where people do. Unable to hear clearly, and confused, my mother-in-law summons her grandson and asks him, anxiously, "Mark, do you know how to speak Jewish?" "Gran," Mark says in his slow, easygoing Floridian way, "there's no such language as Jewish."

Notes

1. At this writing, the legal issues surrounding the case have still not been settled. The man charged with slaying Yankel Rosenbaum was acquitted in a jury trial; after the second trial of the Los Angeles police officers and their conviction on civil rights charges, the Lubavitcher community petitioned for another trial on the violation of Yankel Rosenbaum's civil rights.

2. Brooklyn was an independent city until its absorption as a borough into New York City in 1898.

3. Italians venerate "I dui Giovanni": John F. Kennedy and Pope John Paul the XXIII. Hence "the two Alans."

T h r e e

Slasher Stories

I

They surprise you in quiet places: your doctor's or dentist's office, the couch in your living room, your own bed. They make the world a scary place. They come in every woman's magazine, whether it's devoted to fashion and beauty, home decor and recipes, the problems of young single women, wives, mothers, or career women. They come also in newspapers, especially local newspapers, and on certain segments of the nightly news. I call them slasher stories, though they are not always or just what we traditionally call "slashers"—stories about violence against women by men wielding guns and knives.

The stories I mean make you feel like a victim, a sitting duck—likely to be snuffed out or emotionally devastated at any moment by crime, an accident, disease, a freak of nature. Some examples from a local newspaper of the kind of story I mean: a child strangled while playing with her jump rope; a woman collecting the mail who was torn to bits by her neighbor's pit bulls; a woman hiding with her child in a basement while some men attacked her husband outside the house who held the child so tightly that she suffocated her. These are extreme examples. But they dramatize the essential elements of what I call slasher stories: stories where danger lurks in unexpected places, where routine actions or things (the jump rope, the neighbor's dogs, a mother's embrace) turn deadly, actions that kill or maim the family, actions that are random, arbitrary, unpredictable.

In a way, these stories are more insidious than traditional slashers, which advertise in advance what you are in for—foregrounding fear and showing terror and violence. The stories I am talking about pretend to report the facts or to articulate dangers or, sometimes, to prevent harm—but, more often, what they really do is to create or cause fear. You can't guard against them unless you perfect the art of skipping them in newspapers and magazines and muting them over the television. They're like the ads for horror movies you would never willingly go see, aired between segments of your favorite TV show. Or like boxes in the video store in sections where you don't usually rent, aggressively positioned near the cashier.

Here is how a quiet little story turns into a slasher:

The scene is a haircutter's waiting room. The medium is a house and garden magazine aimed at women of middle income. The story is on fires at home—not "traditional" slasher story material but handled like a classic slasher. There's no real protection, the story says, and this event overtakes you most often at home. Fires are hot, unbelievably hot. Most victims die of gases and heat, not actual contact with the flames, though that's a lurid possibility the article refuses to dismiss. Fire alarms help sound the alert but sometimes don't work or, even when they do, aren't a complete defense. Children upstairs or down? a crippled parent? These people better fend for themselves. Fires are *fast*, the slasher story says. You need to get out, forsaking all others. Everyone needs an escape plan, in fact, several. And everyone needs to take care of him/herself, with a meeting point away from the house, perhaps at a neighbor's, to take a head count.

What happens if a head's missing? This slasher story doesn't dwell on that, though it does say that no one should reenter the burning building. People die all the time trying to save kids who are drinking Kool-Aid at the *other* neighbor's house. This slasher story, like most, loves life's little ironies. And it includes several "personal stories"—the guy who caught his daughter as she jumped from a burning window; the family whose house went up like tinder, thankful for its monthly drills.

Sitting in the waiting room, while my seven- and five-year-olds are having their hair cut, I react as the reader of a good slasher story should. I panic. Within days, before the horror of the slasher story has been forgotten, I've devised a plan—several plans—and run through them with my children. Then an anxiety I haven't had since moving into my solid brick house reasserts itself: our bedroom windows are very small and open awning-style. No great escapes there—and fire alarms might or might not help. I plan renovations. I call the renovators. I buy bigger windows, casement style, big enough to fit through. I make new plans—several plans—and drill the family. The renovator arrives. One night, bedroom in mid-renovation, basketball game on the TV, I'm browsing a standard women's fashion magazine. There it is, the inevitable *counter-slasher-story*, which completes what I call the slasher story double bind.

It too minces no words: we are all in danger—especially women and children—from intruders. Intruders with guns, intruders with knives. Intruders who rape, intruders who murder. Intruders who arrive on Sunday mornings when hubby's at the supermarket with the kids. Or as delivery men. Or through open windows. Or through locked doors. The answer in this slasher story is an alarm system, or a weapon, or—and this takes me full circle—sealed or gated windows, doors with deadbolt locks that unlock from inside only by key. Additions that would make my home a great fire hazard.

II

It might sound, at first, as though the slasher story's main purpose and effect is consumer oriented: to provide business for hardware stores, window salesmen, renovators, and locksmiths. But the slasher story is not, I think, primarily related to selling or buying things. The slasher story primarily appeals to our deepest sense of what it means to be female both inside and out of the home. Slasher stories appeal to the sense that women are vulnerable, physically and emotionally, that women are victims. They do more than appeal—they create and nurture that sense. To explain my reaction to slashers, I need to tell a more complicated story, one that goes back into my childhood home and then forward to my adult one, making excursions to school and several other places along the way. For the dynamics of the slasher story, as I have been describing them, are deeply embedded in what it means in our culture to be a woman.

When I began to do feminist writing, I realized that I was more prone than many other women to look towards men and their values as a source of power and to perceive my affinity for men as protection against the vulnerability of being female. That realization was in itself a little scary, but not really something for which I blamed myself. For these attitudes begin before we have much choice. In my own history, looking towards men begins with being the younger of two children, the sister to my brother, who is the classically spaced two years older than I am. We shared a room until I was pubescent. We shared hours of watching TV and many games based on what we saw. In our Brooklyn childhood, in the alley that separated the building we lived in from that next door, we played games in the snow and the sunshine, often with the three boys who lived next door. We played war a lot, I remember that, building barricades in the alley, firing away in a ghastly imitation of what would happen to one of the neighbor boys less than ten years later in the Vietnam War. We played Robin Hood as well, and cowboys and Indians. In these last games, I sometimes got female roles—Maid Marian, the rancher's daughter, or, when I was lucky, the Indian Princess. My most frequent part in the action was being tied to a stake—to be burned, to be scalped. For this reason, I preferred the war games where I got to be an ordinary soldier or, when reinforcements weren't needed, a nurse. My brother and I had a favorite game, based on a television show called *The Buccaneers.* I loved this game because I got to be an ordinary pirate, not a female stowaway.

From this history of childish play, I would guess I wanted to play male roles early on, though I also accepted and made the best of female ones. I did not completely enter the boys' world of play—I had girls as friends too and organized clinics after dinner on such girlish skills as jumping rope, playing jacks, and ball games like "A my name." I A'd my name the best: "A my name is Alice and my husband's name is Alan and we come from Alabama and we sell—apples." My children have modified this game to exclude the husband's name and give the woman a profession. Its original form was part of why I resisted playing just the female roles—rushing towards an identity that would be subsumed by a husband's, having no profession but his.

In an Italian American household, like the one in which I grew up, the boy comes first. Always did, still does. When I whined and chafed at having to do tasks that my brother did not, my mother's answer was always: "but he's the boy." She probably still wouldn't understand why that answer bothered me. The hidden dynamics of this exchange perhaps governed my relationship with my mother, which I remember as cordial and caring (she was a good mother, the kind who sleeps in your room when you're sick), but also as judgmental and somewhat distant. We never talked much about feelings or sexuality; in fact, our relationship was almost completely devoid of "girl talk." Although she is an excellent cook, she rarely offered to teach me her skills, and when she did, I resisted—as definitely and surely as I resisted, later, learning to type and take shorthand. Similarly, although my mother worked in the garment industry, I myself barely learned to sew, and then only in Home Economics.

My purest moments of female bonding with my mother occurred on shopping trips, on which I remember her generosity and pleasure at making sure I had the clothes I wanted even though it meant straining the family budget. The closeness of these moments was colored, for me, by awareness that the clothes were designed to enhance my attractiveness and my attractiveness my chances of finding a husband. My mother couldn't help valuing me in those terms most of all, and comparing me to prettier, more feminine girls. I wanted something different.

I wanted some of the opportunities available to boys—running for class president, writing for the school newspaper, applying to colleges. It was a boy's world, ultimately, and I knew that. So I tagged along with my brother and his friends all through junior high and high school, hoping to have part of that world, long after they wanted me to get lost and I had acquired close girl friends of my own, who worked on eyebrows and fashions now, not jumping rope and ball games.

The vulnerability of being female was there, but more starkly in my private world than in my public one. I remember being very fearful at night as a child and adolescent, especially after I no longer shared a room with my brother. When I was very young, my parents would tell me that I couldn't keep a light on in our room because the Japanese might see it and bomb the house. This was probably around 1956, and on the East Coast—but what did I know. In retrospect, I think that they told this lie to prevent my brother and me from developing bad habits—and to save money on electric bills. But I am struck by how the desire for the light was expressed by me, not my brother, and also by how I found his presence in the room a psychological comfort. I wonder now if the consequences in dreams were primarily mine as well.

There was a dream I kept having in which the Japanese burst into our apartment and searched for us, room by room. We would be barricaded in the bedroom with the kinds of chairs we used at school blocking the door. It was a scary dream, but in a controlled way that never made me cry out or even tell anyone about it; it was a familiar rhythm in my psychic life. Sometimes the Japanese were Indians, rampaging Apaches. When I got older the intruder was a vampire, a thief, a murderer. I remember sleeping with my hands or covers over my throat or heart so that I could have a few extra seconds to fight the hands or knife that threatened me. These fears and dreams vanished entirely when I got married except when I stayed at a hotel or other unfamiliar place, when I would move, as nonchalantly as possible, a chair in front of the door. That became a joke between my husband and me and now, when traveling has become quite familiar, it's something I haven't even thought of doing in maybe fifteen years. My childhood felt vulnerable; my adult home safe. But I was still open to certain kinds of fears when I was away from home, or on the rare occasions when my husband was.

III

When I was a child, school was an opposite site in my imagination, a light-filled, wide-awake world in which fear did not erupt, except on rare occasions. I saw school as a place where I was valued for my intelligence, even though I was female—

and this probably had something to do with my absence of fear there. I quite naturally chose to stay in school through college and into graduate school. It's in these relatively late years that I first became fully conscious of how even within the world of school I was and always would be female.

I remember especially one occasion, from my first week as a graduate student, in which the slasher story erupted into the usually safe world of school. I had a seminar, with a wiry, cigar-smoking, female professor, in Columbia University's Orals room, a large seminar room decorated with portraits of past professors—stern, unsmiling men whose faces had begun to go (or perhaps always had been) a little green. One of the men in this class volunteered to give the first oral report the very next week. He said it would be on whether or not Charlotte Brontë was a virgin, a subject whose importance he sketched for us at length, pompously. By the end of the course I knew that this man was not the best student or smartest person in the room; yet on that first day he felt entitled to harangue us all and to claim our attention. I felt annoyed at this man's presumption, but also intimidated—as though he must know better than I did what would be expected in graduate school. I felt so out of sync with what was going on around me that I thought perhaps I should drop out of school.

Outside the window of this classroom was another building, lower, and with a flat roof. I fantasized about a guerrilla raid erupting there, with everyone in our room being machine-gunned. I censored the fantasy.

This story gets weirder. After class, I told some of the other women how uncomfortable that man made me, how scary I found him. They found him scary too. One of them told the professor. The next day, I received at home a call from her, asking me if I knew anything about this man, whether he had any kind of history she should know. It seems she was scared too. For a moment I imagined all the women in the room staring out the window at the flat roof next door, seeing terrors. It was like a film that intercuts lurid fantasies with shots of the characters' cool exteriors, functioning like professors and students in a seminar room. It was also a classic instance of one way that women bond together—a negative solidarity formed against an obnoxious and threatening man.

Yet for most of my professional life, I have been only slightly uneasy in wood-paneled rooms with leather chairs, cigar smoke, and portraits of green-tinged male ancestors. I have liked to assume this is because I grew up with men, always had men as nonromantic friends, and always worked with them. For me, work was a refuge from the vulnerability of being female—it provided an identity and an income of my own.

I didn't always feel free to articulate it to myself this way. I liked to think I had drifted into graduate school rather than purposefully going there. For many years, I continued to regard my own career as subordinate to my husband's. He didn't share this view and I believe now that I chose him in part because he didn't. But I couldn't admit that right up front, perhaps because I had been raised in a traditional household where, although my mother worked, all of our anxiety about the family income was focused on my father's job.

I remember once, soon after my marriage, explaining earnestly to my husband my expectation that he would always support me financially. He laughed and disclaimed the role, saying he'd be glad to help but that, once I was out of graduate school, I should be more than able to support myself. Other times, I remember saying that I might easily have become a suburban housewife; he assured me the person he knew had always been ambitious. Even here, in writing this essay, I defer to my husband's authority, use his testimony to prove my case; I feel I need, somehow, a man's permission to enter and remain in the male world of work. Although I am comfortable sitting in the leather chairs, I somehow still believe

I sit there only with various men's consent—my husband's, the senior professors', the Chairman's, or Dean's.

The first time I experienced, really and truly, something other than existing by permission in a male world was when my first child was born. I was aware of the difference and felt that being in the maternity ward was like being locked overnight in the lingerie department of a department store but unexpectedly enjoying it. After visiting hours, when the husbands and doctors went home, it was an all-female world, a women's culture—the first I had ever experienced. The conversation here was about labor, episiotomies, breasts, nursing babies. The female nurses were there to help; my roommate was too. It was a strange but very pleasurable sensation.

I felt most comfortable identifying myself as a female only after I had had a child. I do not mean to say here that motherhood is a woman's destiny, or that only mothers are "real women," or that all mothers feel the same way, or that I identify only or even especially with women who are mothers. I am simply trying to say, as honestly as I can, what was true for me in my experience. For other women, the first positive experience of an all-female world may have come in different ways altogether.

After years now of motherhood, I still think of myself as a woman in this particular way, though no longer as exclusively. I put out my arms at street crossings to guide children—anyone's children. I stop to help kids who seem lost or are crying. In my earlier years, children didn't notice me. Now they do, even if they have never seen me with my own children. I am asked to tie shoelaces, to give tissues, to soothe hurts. I identify myself and am identified as a female in this maternal way. I don't know how it happened or how they know.

Sometimes it seems like an enormous burden, being a woman responsible for the welfare of children. It's like holding a finger in the dike, with the threatening waters the very stuff of slasher stories. I remember when I was a graduate student, studying Latin one summer at the house of a fellow student, an older married woman with three children. She said something I have since noticed to be true with my own children. Her children, she said, would race off the school bus, laughing and joking. As they approached the door, their pace would often slow. They would develop sore throats or other minor illnesses; the complaints of the day would well up. She would kiss foreheads and listen to make it all better, at which point the general cheerfulness would resume. I do the same.

But I always feel a certain uneasiness as I assume the role of unambiguous comforter. My desire to protect and soothe is real. But my abilities seem so small, the threats so large. I learned this first, and for all time, back in the maternity ward after the birth of my first child. Two days after the baby was born, I was told by two male interns, excited by the break in routine, that he had either a severe heart defect or spinal meningitis. (I myself had called a nurse's attention to how loudly the baby's heart beat; in retrospect I felt like a traitor.) I felt the same sort of anger towards these male interns that I felt towards the man in my graduate seminar: lecturing me about the medical possibilities, their cockiness played upon my vulnerability.

My husband rode in an ambulance with our son, Matthew, to Boston; my doctor wasn't available in time to sign me out of the hospital so that I could go too. Then Stu rode back from Boston and drove me home. He hadn't been told much in Boston, except that the doctors would call when they had diagnosed the problem. Once we got home, Stu got into the shower for three hours—he probably wanted to cry, privately, and to adjust to our new situation. Then we waited by the phone, finally calling the hospital when it did not call us. We found out Matthew had a heart defect, and drove three hours to a hospital in Boston so depressing that no adult there wanted to look any other adult in the eye. For two days, while the baby was in intensive care, we slept in hospital corridors; the last day I, as the mother, was allowed to occupy the single bed in the baby's room. Then we were allowed to take the baby home. The prognosis for correcting the defect with surgery was hopeful but guarded, since they had not been able to reach one portion of the heart in catherization. Only now did my husband tell me that the ambulance had crashed on the way to Boston—so that the whole episode had been even more nightmarish than I had known.

We struggled to maintain a steady optimism for the next few months, although each visit back to the hospital in Boston was filled with contradictory signals. On the first, we were criticized for expecting Matthew to grow normally—we had to accept, the doctor said, that our son had a birth defect. We thought we had accepted that, but tried harder. On the second, we were criticized by the same doctor for not having been sufficiently alarmed at the baby's slow rate of growth—growth arrest, the doctor called it—and warned that unless we could make him gain weight they would have to perform surgery sooner than they wanted. I felt bewildered and depressed after each encounter with this male doctor, who cuffed us lightly for not having achieved, in advance, the right combination of attitudes. On each visit, though, we also saw a female nurse-practitioner, who answered our questions and assured us, repeatedly, that we were doing a great job.

This hospital had divided things neatly down the middle: the doctor gave the medical news; the nurse tended psychological needs. The hospital's routine kept male and female stereotypes in place. At the same time, the experience of the hospital disrupted those stereotypes for us: as the parents of a sick baby, my husband and I were both in a vulnerable, dependent role, in thrall to the male doctors. The situation reinforced the redefinition of male-female roles we were attempting at home, where my husband (in accord with our pre-pregnancy agreement) took half of the responsibility for the baby's care.

Back home after this third trip to Boston, we added formula, cereal, and bananas to the baby's diet of breast milk; Matthew cooperated by gobbling everything, looking at us with uncannily serene blue eyes, a wise adult's eyes in an infant's face—the same eyes we had seen in the faces of children at the hospital. We monitored all the signs carefully. One day the signs suggested that our son was in heart failure. We controlled our fear until Stu could have the signs checked by a local nurse-practitioner—I even remember that I kept an appointment to play tennis. It seemed necessary at the time to keep life as normal as possible, not to live each day at a high pitch of crisis since the crisis might last a lifetime. So I played tennis, though I talked the whole time about Matthew. Then my husband and I drove hastily back to Boston, swallowing panic.

This time the doctors were able to do what they felt was a complete diagnosis. The prognosis now was great: two minor defects; two relatively safe surgeries, one now and one in several years, and we should have a completely healthy child. But, we were warned, we had to have surgery done immediately or there would be permanent damage to the lungs. And we shouldn't consider alternative procedures that would correct the problem in one, more intensive surgery, they said, or we would risk brain damage. The doctors were clear and definite; only the nurse-practitioner reminded us, gently, that unexpected things might still happen.

The next day, we waited first in a public room with Muzak grimly repeating "May the Circle Be Unbroken." Then we were allowed a private room, where we read, tenaciously, and whispered worries to each other. After five hours—too long, we both knew—we were told Matthew had died in surgery.

The surgeon who spoke to us sounded shocked—the whole aorta, he said several times, was as thin as a pencil. That meant, I found out later, that the heart was never viable and the baby should, by medical precedent, have died within a few days or, at most, weeks of birth. Matthew's apparent strength had misled the doctors all along. They let us see the baby, very briefly, and with the nurse-practitioner there, in a basement room of the hospital. Then we were on our own, on the streets.

My husband and I decided to drive home from the hospital in Boston, immediately and (on our first confused try) against traffic on the New England Expressway. My bra was soaked with breast milk that was no longer needed. It was devastation.

We had a quiet service at the burial, with just a minister, my parents, brother, and sister-in-law present. My mother had been supremely pleased when I had a child; she felt the loss strongly and was helpful in the week after the baby died. Then she withdrew from the loss, focusing in all my conversations with her on a petty problem in her own life (the threat of eviction from her apartment), perhaps unsure (like almost everyone else) about whether the death of a three-month-old infant should be treated as if it were a stillbirth or like the persistent grief of losing a child. The in-between-ness of the situation and the absence of anyone except my husband to talk to made things much worse. I felt devastated at so many levels—and bereft of my newfound pleasure in being a woman. It was the slasher story in its most mundane, and yet ultimate form—common death disrupting the home.

Twelve years later, this loss can't be thought about all the time—but it's always there. I hover over my children, I warn them of dangers, I knock on wood—but finally, I have to let go. I feel acutely a sense of parental paranoia that I know is also felt by men but is usually verbalized by women.

The first time I wrote about my first child's illness and death, I left out my husband's part in the story; then I realized the omission was part of the slasher story syndrome, which decrees that only women and children are victims. Like me, my husband felt the deepest possible grief. In fact, for months after the baby's death, we needed to keep each other in sight and panicked when one of us was missing. It was a visceral feeling that still surfaces at times: full of fear—not of fires or men with knives, but of being alone, unloved, bereft. Like being that kid in bed with her hands over her throat, only emotionally now, afraid of grief, not violence.

The slasher story codes "home" as female and dangerous intruders as male. The truth is tougher than that. Home is a site of vulnerability for all of us—men, women, and children. Home is the last frontier.

IV

The common theme that runs through these memories is that women feel a solidarity with pain and suffering—physical violence or psychic stress, or sometimes, in the details of day-to-day life, just putting other people's needs first. There's a submotif that sometimes things go wrong and that it's a woman's job to give solace and comfort, and to make them go right. These motifs are conventional in a way. Freud and his followers believed that women were defined by their grievance at biological "deficiencies"; Freudian Helen Deutsch defined "normal" femininity as a mixture of passivity and masochism.[1] I have always hated these classic psychoanalytic views though, of course, orthodox Freudians would claim that my conscious denial points all the more to my unconscious belief.[2] Yet I still maintain it would be more accurate to say not that women are biologically or psychically destined for suffering and pain, but

that they are more inclined, culturally, to verbalize those feelings.[3]

In the summer of 1990, I taught a literature class for high
school students. At one class, the topic of Conrad's views of
women came up and I went (for these high school students)
further than I had meant to go in showing how Conrad con-
nects women to the themes of violence and death that haunt
the male-dominated world of *Heart of Darkness*.[4] I wanted to
disrupt stereotypes about men and women and spoke with
what I thought was confidence. Afterwards, the perkiest of the
young men stayed behind to talk. He said he felt sorry for
women—they had so much pain, with periods and childbirth.
They worried so much and complained so much to each other.
The two women who had also lingered and I began to shake
our heads. He replied immediately to our implied criticism,
"Men aren't like that." When they get together, he said
proudly, they "rag" each other, really "tear each other up"
with mock insults. Exactly, I said, that was the point; might it
not be better to "bolster and fluff" our friends rather than
"tear them up"?

When I think about the metaphors my male student and I
used, the connection between slasher stories and male or
female roles becomes clearer. Men are taught to compete and
to endure pain in sports and in "the rough stuff" of boyish
play. They learn to "rag" and "tear each other up" conversa-
tionally—a devastating, though bloodless, scene. Women play
household games and learn to fluff each other up—the domestic activity of bed making. But of course these metaphors are
false—and at times reversible. Women can "rag" and "tear
each other up"—in gossip, or in competition over work or
domestic prowess. Men feel pain and discouragement too,
though they usually (like women) bare them only to females if
they can bare them at all.

In fact, I have always felt a little sorry for men in the strict patriarchal system. A few other women have confessed the same feeling, and in almost identical terms that have to do with memories of their father's discomfort with work and their mother's anxiety about the family's income. To have all the responsibility for the family's success, to be the family's link to the world, to be forbidden the outlet of tears, seems a powerful burden. Men are so vulnerable to public failure and disgrace, and so forbidden to show it. They tend most easily to express not pain, but anger.[5]

Since the sixties, feminism has emphasized, and rightly, the oppressiveness of women's confinement at home. Yet the view from the other side, in which home is a refuge from the world of work, is also true.[6] In traditional jobs and families, away from 8:00 to 6:00, men reenter the home as strangers, into space already occupied by wives and children. Women at home fear slashers. But in a different way, men too rarely have the safe and unguarded experience of being home alone.

When our first child was born, my husband was a graduate student; since he was not in a conventional job, he was able to spend large amounts of time with the baby. That was part of the irony of the baby's death. By the time our second and third children were born, he was a stockbroker, working on commission and expected to be at the office all day and after dinner and even on weekends. I resented being not just a worker but also responsible for the second shift at home;[7] in turn, he would have liked to take some of the responsibilities at home. I thought I had the worst of the bargain. But now I remember an argument one night in which Stu said he sometimes felt like he ought to live on the porch—that he had no real place in our home, no time with the children, no time for real friends—and that "our" world was really mine. The feeling he expressed is, I believe, a common experience for men who work long hours—the normal mode in our culture.

I know women get abused by men all the time, in big ways

and small—at business meetings, by catcalls on the street, in the division of duties or (in the worst cases) in violence at home. So I feel angry at men, especially at controlling men like the doctors in this story, but also sorry for them.

The slasher story in its purest form—man with knife, hurting women—almost seems like revenge exacted for men's inner rage, the public decorum, the way that women must seem to them, sometimes, to float free of men in the protected space of friendship and home, the way that men must sometimes feel locked out of that space. So it's the very essence of the slasher story to violate that space, as it violates the woman's body. It's not just the transposition of penis for knife that's at work, but the transposition of woman's body for the protected space of home, with both creating a rage of exclusion.

V

Sitting on the couch, remote control in hand, have you ever whisked through the channels, sound off? If you have, you may have seen what I have. Channel after channel in which women are portrayed in ways that seem, somehow, ominous. One night, especially exhausted, I was doing that turn through the channels. One channel showed an unusual image for television: the naked body of a slim, handsomely muscled man, shown full view from behind, standing in a bathroom. I lingered for perhaps five seconds, curious about the context. I was sorry I did.

Retracting the muting command, the first sound I heard was a whimpering woman and the man's voice, saying over her whimpers and pointing to the shower stall—Why didn't you tell me he was there? The music was discordant, jagged, staccato, scary. The next shot was of a different woman, not in the lighted bathroom, but in a darkened nearby bedroom, looking terrified. I knew now that I had stumbled into a slasher story. But it was too late. We were already back in the bathroom, with the whimpering woman curled on the bathroom floor, badly bloodied. The man, shown now from the waist up, had the front of his body smeared with blood, and he was holding a knife. The "he" of the dialogue was apparently someone else, hiding in the shower stall, whom the slasher had just done away with. The woman on the floor was clearly next. At this point, disgusted, I switched to the next channel. But I found myself coming back to this show twice more.

The first time, I saw the face of the woman in the bedroom, still terrified, listening to the moans from the bathroom; when the moans ominously ceased, she plunged desperately under the bed as a hiding place. The second time the slasher was in the bedroom, knife in hand, looking for something on the floor, but not yet seeing, not yet finding the woman under the bed. At this point I shut off the TV and stopped looking.

The mega-visual moment this TV show evoked is, of course, the shower scene in Alfred Hitchcock's *Psycho*. I first saw *Psycho* when I was about thirteen, on one of my first babysitting jobs. Afterwards I had to walk two long blocks and take a bus home. I was terrified, palms sweating, heart beating intensely. For years afterwards, I was afraid in the hallway of our building. I would hurry through it to the door, casting a glance backward towards the cubby that led to the basement. Sometimes I would imagine the Anthony Perkins' character from *Psycho*, dressed as his mother, lurching out, not exactly after me, but close enough to make it feel good when I had opened the outside door and was out in the open air.

The show alluded as well to a real mass murder: the Richard Speck case, in which eight nurses were murdered, one by one, by the knife-wielding Speck; a ninth nurse escaped by hiding under a bed and then climbing out a window to get help. The murders occurred twenty-five years ago; I know because there was a newspaper article about the anniversary in July of 1991, shortly before Speck died of a heart attack.[8] The newspaper story brought back in a flash my fascinated horror with the event when I was sixteen, pouring over the maps of the nurses' apartment that the newspapers printed and reprinted, marked with x's where the police had found the bodies.

A former graduate student named Helen Robbins, with whom I had lunch the day after the anniversary story appeared, remembered reading at the time that nurses are a special target of male violence: the mother figure; the woman in a white uniform; the symbol of female authority and a man's need for women's help. That observation tallied, I noted, with work by Theweleit on male fascists, in which the idealization of the nurse is poised on the knife-edge of violence.[9] Robbins went on to say that the way Speck committed the murders, taking the women, one by one, to their deaths, probably depended on the nurses' willingness to take orders from male doctors, and to do so without question. She thought it odd that the nurses didn't jointly attack their murderer, a single man with a knife. She was of course right, and her intention was not to "blame the victim" for the crime, but to point out how women seem to need male permission, even to save their own lives.

Like *Psycho,* the Speck story resides in our imaginations as an unwrapped parable of male-female relations.[10] Men and women alike find it repugnant and yet fascinating. In the popular imagination, it could only be overshadowed by an event like the Manson murders—in which the most celebrated victim was, of course, the pregnant Sharon Tate—murders committed, this time, by women with knives, following male orders.

The conventional explanations for these events, and for our fascination with them, is that irrationality will out and that we need these public spectacles as a form of catharsis. Freud theorized that the need to control violence was the mainspring for civilized law and religion; in this view, there's an innate desire for violence in the human psyche (Freud focused on males) that finds expression in acts of this kind or in fantasies like the Oedipal parricide.[11] Freud also believed that war was a reversion to "primitive" aggression at the level of nations and civilizations.[12] Men supposedly psychically crave violence, and women to submit to it, so that violence is built into current equations for masculinity and femininity whether we like it or not.[13] The rigidity of roles and attitudes embedded in these views seems regrettable, but somehow inevitable. To keep our account of horrors neat and tidy, we code violence as "male"; victimization and fear as "female"—the same neat but deceptive coding that exists in the slasher story.

Even within a changing social world, we still do body and mind checks to see that we conform to norms deemed male or female. Aware of the crossings of male and female identification within us all, we still deny them. We live the stereotypes even as we try to alter them. Psychologies like Jung's remain marginalized curiosities as compared to Freud's—perhaps because Jung so firmly believed in "maleness" and "femaleness" within us all, and especially in changing roles over time and through aging. In fact, Jung believed that one function of middle and old age was to unlearn the male or female identification that had been the primary business of young adult life.[14]

My own choice to think of men, or men's good opinions, or my own professionalism as protection against being female was thus doomed to failure. For the syndrome of male versus female identification, like the dichotomy of work and home, poses only two extremes, not modulating possibilities. I was never really *male-identified*—that is, I never wanted to be the one committing violence. I just wasn't *female-identified,* the one willing to be the victim. I couldn't buy the notions I grew up with of what being female meant; I can't buy now the notion of what being male means. Experience tells me that it's all more complicated than these terms indicate; yet there are few models for anything else. This leaves me, in the cultural scheme of things, nowhere. It is a double bind, a no-win situation—not unlike that produced by the two conflicting slasher stories with which I began.

NOW THAT I HAVE WRITTEN about the fears, have I contained them? Well—yes—I feel better, but also—no.

Does talking about danger court it? Reason says, Of course not. But I am a child of the *malòcchio*—the Italian evil eye; I understand the *kine-ahora*, the Yiddish "God forbid!" I grew up with charms shaped like humpbacks carrying a horseshoe in one hand and forking the fingers of the other hand to turn back ill wishes on the wisher; I understand red ribbons tied to baby carriages to ward off envious or malicious eyes. Deep down I hope that talking about danger prevents it, that airing fears will dissipate the conditions that cause fear. As I finish this essay, I knock on wood.

Notes

1. The classic texts are Sigmund Freud, "Female Sexuality," *Standard Edition of the Complete Psychological Works of Sigmund Freud*, trans. James Strachey, 24 vols. (London: Hogarth, 1953–74), vol. 21; Sigmund Freud, "Femininity," *New Introductory Lectures in Psychoanalysis*, trans. and ed. James Strachey (1939; rpt. New York: Norton, 1965); Helene Deutsch, *The Psychology of Women*, 2 vols. (New York: Grune and Stratton, 1944), 45.

2. More recent psychologists disavow Freud and Deutsch's theories. See, for example, Jean Baker Miller, M.D., ed., *Psychoanalysis and Women* (Baltimore: Penguin, 1973).

3. On women's propensity for "troubles talk," see Deborah Tannen, *You Just Don't Understand: Men and Women in Conversation* (New York: Morrow, 1990).

4. I was reprising my interpretation in *Gone Primitive: Savage Intellects, Modern Lives* (Chicago: University of Chicago Press, 1990).

5. In its overly simple, sometimes silly, but still impressive way, that is a major point of Robert Bly's *Iron John: A Book about Men* (Reading, Mass.: Addison-Wesley, 1990), a phenomenon of the current men's movement. I especially liked its chapter about grief, "The Road of Ashes, Descent, and Grief."

6. On the modulating effects of these conceptions of home as prison and refuge, see Barbara Ehrenreich and Deidre English, *For Their Own Good: 150 Years of Experts' Advice to Women* (New York: Doubleday, 1979).

7. See Arlie Russell Hochschild, *The Second Shift: Working Parents and the Revolution at Home* (New York: Viking, 1989).

8. Here and at other points in the essays, I have retained time indicators appropriate to when each essay was originally written. "Slasher Stories," for example, was originally written between 1988 and 1991.

9. Klaus Theweleit, *Male Fantasies: Women, Floods, Bodies, Histories.* vol. 1, trans. Stephen Conway, in collaboration with Erica Carter and Chris Turner (Minneapolis: University of Minnesota Press, 1987).

10. Carol Clover suggests that slasher films after *Psycho* often provide a female hero for the audience to identify with—"the final girl" originally slated for victimhood, who succeeds in killing the murderer by mastering his methods. The model works for films such as *Terminator* and *Terminator II.* See Carol J. Clover, "Her Body, Himself: Gender in the Slasher Film," *Representations* 20 (Fall 1987), 187–228.

11. See Sigmund Freud, *Totem and Taboo,* trans. James Strachey (1913; rpt. New York: Norton, 1950) and *Civilization and Its Discontents,* trans. James Strachey (1930; rpt. New York: Norton, 1961).

12. See Sigmund Freud, "Why War?" in *Collected Papers,* vol. 5, ed. James Strachey (London: Hogarth, 1950).

13. In some descriptions of heterosexual intercourse from Helen Deutsch to Catherine MacKinnon, violence, pornography, and "normal" sex are seen as structurally equivalent, regardless of emotional content. See Catherine A. MacKinnon, *Towards a Feminist Theory of the State* (Cambridge: Harvard University Press, 1989).

14. Carl Jung, "The Stages of Life," in *The Portable Jung,* ed. Joseph Campbell (London: Penguin, 1976), 18–22. The contemporary men's movement, which draws heavily on Jung, wobbles as Jung

does on whether there are, or are not, emotional states essentially male and female. In *Fire in the Belly: A Book about Men* (New York: Bantam, 1991), Sam Keen finesses the problem by saying that everything men feel—from conventionally male emotions like anger to conventionally female emotions like the desire to nurture children—should be considered male. It's a nice formulation, but doesn't answer the basic question.

F o u r

The College Way

I

When I moved to a college town in New England I bought a bra. I bought sweaters, hats, and gloves too, in preparation for the cold climate. But to ensure my professionalism as a new assistant professor, I bought a bra, previously perceived, in the early seventies, as unnecessary for my small-breasted figure. It was precisely the kind of compromise destined not to work.

The town I lived in is a small, wealthy village. Of its three thousand permanent residents, more than one third teach or work at the College, so that life in the community is pretty much the same thing as academic life. The town centers around Main Street, a wide, grand promenade, lined by huge trees and old, large, stately houses. Stores cluster on a single street, which always looks pretty much the same even though businesses come and go. One man, returning to the town after thirty years, said, in bemusement, that except for the cars and fashions it still could be the nineteen-fifties. Still could.

I lived in one quarter of a huge white house on a hill five

miles outside the town. It was a mansion that had originally been built for workers on the large estate across the road, which was once owned by a Rockefeller. There were a river, cornfields, cows, apple orchards, and banks of lilacs all around our house, which overlooked a huge green lawn roughly the size of a football field. From our front porch, we could see mountains. It was a bucolic setting, evocative of nineteenth-century beauty and grace. The house and grounds were owned and carefully manicured by the College, which rented apartments in the house to new faculty members.

The College itself is one of the most elite of small liberal arts colleges. Its faculty is hardworking and devoted to teaching; its students smart and well connected. It is not uncommon to be talking to a sweet undergraduate about Mom and Dad and to find out that Dad is an Episcopal Bishop or the Secretary of State. That's the kind of place the College is—a small place whose connections have, over the years, proved wide and strong.

The setting in a mountain valley is wonderfully beautiful. On three sides, the valley is ringed by mountains that turn purple when the sun sets, especially when they are bare or snow-covered, which is the case for approximately eight months of the year. Icy, mountainous roads often make driving difficult and dangerous, isolating residents. The nearest small city has a population of less than 100,000. The nearest large town is an ugly twin to the college town, a former mill town as thoroughly working class and ethnic as the college town is upper middle class and WASP.

When I was invited to a job interview at the College, I boarded a bus at the Port Authority Terminal in Manhattan; a true New Yorker, I neither owned a car nor knew how to drive. I asked the bus driver repeatedly when we would get to the town, since I had the geography all wrong. Within a year it would seem shocking to me that anyone would never have heard of the town or the College. An assistant professor once said that after a while in the community ("the happy valley," a friend and I called it) the world becomes a rumor. But as a big-city kid I had not heard of the College or thought about such places until I was asked to come up for an interview.

When I accepted the job and called the suave owner of our Brooklyn Heights brownstone to explain why we would be leaving our apartment, *his* recognition was instant. More, he treated me with new respect—hadn't realized that he housed so intellectually distinguished a tenant. Then he announced that the owner of the brownstone next door, a banker, was an alumnus, no, a trustee, of the College. I knew I had made it to the big time and began to get anxious about my lack of the proper underwear.

Over the next four years, my education into the local laws of conduct was more or less completed. I learned that my underwear, however impeccable, would not do under the jeans and sweaters I wore regularly to class. I learned to buy properly demure, classic dresses, skirts, and blouses. I perceived that dinner invitations must be extended to newcomers—once, though usually only once, as they had been extended to me— and at regular intervals to continuing faculty. I learned to eat meals using silverware from the outside in. I learned not to curse in the matter-of-fact way New Yorkers do and not to be rude to local merchants who took longer than I expected at the cash register. I learned to avoid seeming surprised when people on campus showed less interest in, say, Jimmy Carter's abortive attempt to rescue hostages in Iran than in a change in the date of finals week that year. I tried to fit in and mostly did though the total fit could never be achieved. There was something about my intellectual style or maybe my emotional style that just didn't work: they knew it, I knew it.

For example, at freshman convocation, an administrator talked to students about coming to college from prep school or secondary school and how it would affect their lives. "Nothing will change," he said to the bright eager freshmen, opening his arms out wide, "the College will see to that." Remembering my own restless youth—remembering even the usual clichés of convocation speeches or the ambition of colleges to educate their students—the statement boggled my imagination. But it was typical of what could go wrong in this particular setting. The College prided itself on good manners, excellence, and a sense of social responsibility—the finest Yankee values. While it achieved these goals with some consistency, other things slipped in: a sense of entitlement and complacency, insularity, an aversion to rocking the boat.

The curious thing is that the town hid nothing. It announced itself clearly, loud and strong, although I was too young and naive to hear what was being said. On my first visit, I was given a quick tour and description: everyone called it "the quintessential college town," but I didn't know what that meant. People alluded to how Edward Albee's *Who's Afraid of Virginia Woolf?* had been based on a notorious situation at the College. I had seen the play, but still the potential viciousness below the surface of the place didn't sink in: I only thought it curious that perfectly nice seeming people would willingly compare themselves and their town to the characters and setting of the play.

My welcoming dinner was a rite of passage. Everyone else had gin and water before dinner—several in most cases. I had never seen anyone drink gin and water and opted for a single glass of wine. At dinner, I was treated to knowing allusions to adultery in *Ulysses* and to several mentions of how it was a shame my husband had not come with me on this initial visit—the town's social life running, I was told, to "couples."

In retrospect, some of the welcoming rituals appear cruel beneath their genteel surface. One man, for example, regularly gave charades parties to welcome new assistant professors. I had never played charades and at first it seemed like fun. Did I know what *The Abduction from the Seraglio* was (luckily I did) and could I act it out in a dignified way (I couldn't and opted for the obvious belly dance); what was "Barkis is willing" (it's a tag phrase from Dickens' *David Copperfield*) and could it be guessed without getting down on hands and knees and imitating a barking dog (as it turned out, it couldn't be guessed at all). Why do I remember these specific charades, which fell to me, so many years later? Surely because they were intended at some level to test and humiliate me, and they succeeded.

When my husband's sister, a veteran of living in upwardly mobile suburbias came to visit us, she said something I found curious at the time. Noting all the invitations we were receiving she said: don't be surprised if all that stops; don't be surprised if they don't mean it; don't be surprised if these people aren't like us. She was right, though I was puzzled by her warnings at the time. This town didn't come through for me when I needed it most and I have never been able to forgive it.

I was at this College when my first child was born with a defective heart. I was only the second woman faculty member to have a baby at this college, and the first untenured one. So it was important to me that this birth be a model of professionalism. The baby was due in May, with only two classes to go until the end of the semester; I had taught sessions in advance to avoid canceling classes, and so on. For the first two days after my son Matthew was born, everything seemed perfect and right on schedule. Then, the day we were to return home from the local hospital, the doctors discovered a heart defect and rushed the baby to a hospital in Boston.

My husband and I were caught up in a sea of emotions and the suspense of what would prove to be an ever-changing diagnosis. At the hospital, I concentrated intently on the baby and didn't think about the College. I made a "fate-bet"—a one-sided bargain with a noncommital God, something very Italian: if the baby lived through intensive care and got to come home, he would live—no matter what; if he were going to die, he would die then and not later on. A week later, we were allowed to return home with our son. I felt euphoric, even though I knew he faced major surgery.

Back in town, euphoria collided with the realities of adjusting to my new position in the college town. I was no longer an efficient though pregnant professor. I was now the mother of a sick child—and connected with something that many people in the town found hard to confront. Some people simply pretended that nothing special had happened. Even people who didn't self-consciously avoid the topic often touched the wrong chords. I can see now that my brisk "business as usual" attitude was partly to blame and made it hard for people to get their tones right. But I don't think that was all that was happening.

One long-term resident, whose son also had a birth defect, said to me that the college town can be a difficult place to have misfortune or be unhappy. As if in a grand Calvinist scheme, good fortune seems to confirm merit; bad fortune seems to suggest something else, from which people avert their eyes, politely. The town never articulated these values to itself, except indirectly. It was not unusual, for example, for people to note that the faculty and students were an unusually good-looking group of people. Indeed, in six years of teaching, I had only one undergraduate who was pimply or overweight. This would be remarkable if it were accidental. But it probably reflected assumptions at the admissions office that went something like this: good looks and intelligence go along with good health and good fortune; they make people "well rounded"; they suit "the College way." But then "the College way" collided with my son's illness.

My first telephone call after getting home was from a faculty wife who had recently earned her Ph.D. but did not have a job teaching college. She expressed sympathy for the baby's condition and told me that her first baby had been hospitalized too, though for something more minor. So far, so good. I felt the muscles in my neck begin to relax into her sympathy. Then she went on to say that to her I had seemed to have everything—a career as well as a family—and that now this "tragedy" made it seem "ironic" that she had envied me. I was in no mood for "tragedy"—much less "irony." I felt pierced by the multiple ways that her empathy was working—by her hint of competition—and I felt my body stiffen in resistance. Fortunately, the next call was from a friend who drove right over with a baby gift—and that felt good.

A bubbly man, nearer to my age and one of my closer friends in the town, was thinking of starting a family, as Stu and I had, after a long and deliberate period of married childlessness. He babbled the first day he saw me: "I'm glad the baby is home. We were thinking about you. You know that could have happened to us. We could actually be in your situation. Wouldn't that be awful? Did you think about that? Did you?" Actually, I hadn't, nor had I ever really thought to myself—as he and many other people insisted I must have— why couldn't this have happened to someone else?

Matthew died in surgery when he was three months old. It was early July. Most of the students were gone, most of the faculty still in town.

After the death notice in the newspaper, some people actually crossed the street rather than talk to me. A few of my colleagues called, but most just sent notes. Some didn't even mention the death and never have. Social invitations tapered off dramatically. My bubbly friend and his wife continued the invitations but only, I was told, if I promised not to cry, even in private conversations.

It was a hurtful time. But I was aware even then that not everyone was cruel. A student biked out the five miles to my house to present a cake, her face streaming with tears. Some people were there, week after week, just to listen. A faculty couple with an autistic child invited us to their beach house, knowing it might help, as they put it, "to be under a different sky." It was the contact, the willingness to share our company, that made these gestures right. Still, all in all, it was a wretched and isolated period. Invitations only resumed after my second baby was born. By that time, I had lost my taste for the college town and begun a job search that brought me to North Carolina and Duke in 1981.

II

For about twelve years after my first baby died, I experienced grief at regular intervals—shorter and further apart, as is typical, but still acute. I talked about the death with some people, but never in much detail until I wrote this essay and "Slasher Stories." Matthew's death was not exactly a secret, but it was something extremely personal that I wanted to share only with people who would understand how important it was and would not forget what they had been told—as people often did. Sometimes I surprised myself by tears as I sat at my desk reconstructing events and emotions as accurately as possible. The writing made my grief not less real, but less raw.

Yet I find I have still not told the full story of my life in the college town because I have kept another kind of secret: the fact that I did not get tenure at this first job. Everything in my profession urges secrecy; mostly, I have kept the secret, sometimes even from friends. Even now, years after I have been tenured and promoted to full professor, an occasional colleague (feeling mean, or intimate, or both) alludes darkly to knowing about what happened in the college town. I always think of my dead baby—until I realize that they mean not getting tenure. In the same way, over the years, when I have told an academic friend about Matthew's death, surprisingly often I have gotten a tenure story in return—as though they or someone else had died in being denied tenure.

These two things occurred in sequence in my life: losing the baby, being denied tenure. I do not believe that I ever confused anger at not getting tenure with grief over Matthew. So I have puzzled over the way that other academics sometimes substitute not getting tenure for death. Now I think I understand.

The tenure process is surrounded by talk of "judgments," "destinies," and "fates." It makes departments feel powerful; it makes candidates feel vulnerable and exposed. Departments that deny someone tenure feel they have committed murder— and they want to bury the corpse. The analogy between death and tenure is not, of course, really valid. I suspect it may not even make sense to anyone but academics—because people get fired and get new jobs all the time, but dead people don't come back. Still, I experienced the process leading up to tenure as a sustained attack on my identity and self-esteem— something that, like the pain of my baby's death, had to be endured and survived day by day. At that level, but only at that level, I can understand the substitution of tenure for death narrative.

Every day, on campuses large and small, preparing for tenure haunts new teachers, wearing them down for years and years, sometimes damaging them beyond repair. It's a painful process, unnecessary in the long run. I want to recall what it was like to be an assistant professor in a place like the college town, marked for departure several years down the line.

BEFORE I WAS HIRED AT THE COLLEGE, I was told that I was part of an expanded search to replace an extremely popular male teacher whose firing had been controversial. The first search had produced the then-chairman's spouse as a leading candidate; an evenly split vote in the department had led the College administration to try again. I emerged as the preferred candidate on the second round. The situation was, obviously, dangerous. If I had had another offer, I would have taken it. But this was in a year with a terrible job market, and one I had entered late in the year. I took the job, expecting some problems, but also expecting that I could prove myself in five years' time. I decided that, if the lay of the land were indeed treacherous, I would leave at the end of my fourth year, before the tenure process began.

Five years proved a spit in the bucket. When they were over, my rival was still around. Later, this person would be hired by the College; some people on campus had even referred to my position as this person's job while I held it. My plan to leave at the end of my fourth year would have been a good idea, but went awry when my baby died the summer before that academic year. That fall, I did not feel able to mount a job search or make major decisions; all I wanted was to get pregnant again as quickly as possible. So I stayed on through the tenure process, which at the time was based solely on internal evaluation. Though I asked for evaluations by experts outside the College, of the kind normally sought for tenure review, I was told that the College would not itself request such letters, and would consider any letters I solicited as biased.

The year I was hired, three other assistant professors were hired in my department as well; from the very first weeks, we were put in lock step. Like all "junior faculty," we four were treated as a "class"—much in the way that the freshmen at the convocation were taught to identity with their "year." To college insiders, this abundance of new assistant professors promised no good. Only one or (in a most unusual year) two could be kept: an isolated college, the line ran, needs continual new blood.

From the time of our arrival onwards, the College went out

of its way to make it clear who would fit and who would not—this was, I believe, its own attempt to be fair. Distinctions between assistant professors would be made right up front: for example, in the order of lunch or dinner invitations (these sometimes listed in departmental memos), or in extremely small salary differences. For some, there was an almost systematic "Other-izing" that was at least partly ethnic. For example, during the first few years, I was repeatedly mistaken by people at the College for a Jewish woman in the religion department who was much shorter, much thinner, had different color eyes and long curly hair while mine was shoulder length and straight. The same thing happened to an Irish friend with short hair who joined the faculty shortly after I did. Finally, I asked someone why there was all this confusion. The explanation was that the religion professor, my Irish friend, and I "all had dark hair and were 'exotic' looking." It seemed like a classic case of "them" all looking alike.

But the real issue was not, I think, ethnicity or even gender. In fact, there were some ethnic professors who had made a career of acting out an idea of WASPdom and enforcing "the College way." All three of the women mistaken for each other were marked for departure. For some people, a kind of academic triage required that we not in any real way be seen. We did not truly "look alike"—but we were perceived the same way by people in the college town.

The College had many habits and traditions that looked collegial and egalitarian. For example, "junior" (untenured) people evaluated "senior" (tenured) people's classes, and senior people evaluated junior people's classes—as though the situations were parallel. Yet when untenured people observed tenured professors' classes, they knew they were expected to gush enthusiastically—while senior people had a full range of options. I was a successful teacher. But I noticed that even when I had had a great class, praise would be brief, criticism long. I resented this. I felt as if everything were being arranged to make the tenure decision to come seem natural and inevitable—to make my colleagues feel good about the decision they already knew they would make.

The same system was imposed with regard to publishing: what those to be denied tenure wrote had to be criticized. We had regular colloquia at which certain people's papers would be lavishly praised and others ruthlessly savaged. It will sound strange, but it is true that assistant professors in my department at this time were actively discouraged from writing books and told to aim for "one or two stunning articles" instead—as though publishing books damaged teaching. Only outside reassurances kept people who published on track; and only publication saved their careers once things had run their course.

My time at the College taught me some bad lessons about writing that it took years to unlearn. Sharon O'Brien has described academic writing as like building an armadillo: an armored shell designed to repel criticisms that one sets gingerly before colleagues to run for its life. That was how I experienced academic writing at the College. After some devastating criticisms, I would stay in bed the next day, the covers drawn up over my face.

The fall I was up for tenure, I knew I had to go on the job market aggressively. It was a good year, personally and professionally. I had recently had a healthy baby girl. My first book was out and got strong early reviews. I had begun my second book, though its topic (art and literature), my colleagues assured me, was "too big" for someone the likes of me. "Geniuses work on topics like that," the bubbly colleague said, shaking his head over my prospects. That same year, to my surprise, I was nominated for a prestigious fellowship, applied, and won. I was feeling fairly confident about the future when I was told I had been denied tenure.

When I was told the news, I was offered a characteristic arrangement: if I left quietly, no one at the College would mess up my search for a new job by saying that the tenure decision had already taken place; I would be free to say that I was leaving completely on my own initiative. If I used the College's appeal system or sued, anybody asking for a recommendation would have to be told I had not gotten tenure. I felt as if they were taking away my rights and threatening me—and asking for my complicity. I felt invited into what I call the "Dewey Dell syndrome," after the character in Faulkner's *As I Lay Dying* who believes that if no one says out loud that she's pregnant, then she really isn't. Oddly enough, Italian Americans also believe that not saying something aloud allays the truth; I call it faith in euphemism. I was angry and aggressive. But I also knew that I didn't really want to stay at the College. So I took the deal.

III

Recently I returned to the college town to show my older daughter where she was born—and also to assess my feelings. I was a visiting professor in the Northeast, I was writing this essay, and coming to terms with the college town seemed like a case of "now or never." It turned out to be both.

The town was still pristine and beautiful—more beautiful than I had remembered, with the bluest blues and greenest greens, and an amazing sky in which every star shines forth with startling clarity. Surprisingly little had changed: the general store, the gas stations, a gift shop, even the laundromat, just where they had been and owned by the same families. It was still a picture-postcard kind of place—lovely and peaceful. I felt a general sense of forgiveness, but also—I can't deny it— a certain spite. During the visit, I pointed at a newspaper where there was an ad for nose jobs and quipped to my husband, "Know what this place reminds me of? The 'after' photograph." It was a funny remark but it also told me that while my vendetta with the college town had abated, it had never ended.

On the trail of nostalgia, my husband and I revisited old haunts. We were amazed at how little time it took to show our children all the things that we had for years regarded as prime entertainment: a lovely walk along a river, a drive through the mountains, a pottery shop, the K-Mart in the town next door. The trip turned out to be a very pleasant experience—pleasant, like the town itself. *Amiable,* in the way Jane Austen uses the word in *Pride and Prejudice* (which I taught there): possessing a necessary civility that can become, over time, a certain shallowness.

We saw no one we wanted to avoid. We did see our few real friends in the college town, people I treasure. On our last day, my younger daughter looked around and said, "Don't you just love white picket fences?" Then she asked—what I knew she was thinking—about some day applying to the College. It gave me pause, imagining. I finally replied, "Well, Elizabeth, we'll see [a formula she has probably learned to translate as "probably not"]. It *is* nice here. But you know, there are *lots* of pretty college towns."

PART TWO

Readings by an Italian American Daughter

F i v e

Dr. Dolittle and the Acquisitive Life

I

I'm at the supermarket, at the checkout counter, looking around for something to read to pass the time. My eye skips mechanically over the candy bars and chewing gum. On the way to *Vogue* and *Glamour,* it pauses at a section filled with paperbacks, many for children. Among the books is the jewel of children's books, *The Story of Doctor Dolittle.* My heart leaps up as my hand reaches out to put this treasure in my shopping cart.

I have looked for this book before, only to be told it was out of print; other parents probably have looked too, and their requests led Dell Yearling Books to begin republication in a moderately priced format. Dell planned eight volumes between 1988 and 1992. Brisk sales accelerated the schedule. Thanks to Dell, I have had the pleasure of reading these books aloud to my children. Night after night, over months that stretched into years, we read the adventures of Dr. Dolittle, that tenderhearted man who studies animal languages and talks with his menagerie of animal friends—a duck named Dab-Dab, a dog named Jip, a pig named Gub-Gub, a parrot named Polynesia, and others. The children laughed. My younger daughter, in bed for the readings, skipped out of bed each time I held up a picture, to come closer—"I want to see that," she said, "Oh, *cute.*"

I remember the books vividly from childhood. In fact, for me possessing *Doctor Dolittle* had become, through the accidents of memory, a synecdoche for the whole process of owning books. Unlike my children, I did not have books of my own until well into my teens, and even then my collection was meager (Edna St. Vincent Millay, an anthology of American poems, one of short stories, Helen Keller's autobiography, a few plays by Shakespeare, and not much more). The first book I almost owned was in the Dolittle series. I took it out of the library in the first grade—*Dr. Dolittle's Post Office,* to be precise—and I loved it, especially its simple line drawings of the good Doctor and his animal friends. I loved it so much I neglected to return it to the library, incurring my first overdue fines. The fines were heavy—some $1.25—at the time, a fortune. My parents were angry—or at least that's how I remember it. They talked about not letting me take any more books from our public library but relented on that. Then they talked about how maybe the fines would equal the cost of a lost book and maybe I should just keep the book. I held my breath in anticipation. Ultimately, the fines did not equal the replacement cost and the book went back. But my love for Doctor Dolittle and my desire to own him linked my childhood to this moment in the supermarket.

The book is exactly as I remember it. The line drawings are still charming, the cover is the same, one of the drawings from the particular novel framed by a kaleidoscope of motifs from them all, mostly line drawings of the Doctor's pudgy profile or of his animal friends. The experience of reading Doctor Dolittle is even better now than it was in my childhood, since we (my children and I) get to read the books in order.

It's all there, as I remember it. The good Doctor loves the animals and cares for them; they love him and help him out of numerous scrapes. It's Edenic all around except that his human practice drops off as he becomes obsessed with his animals, and the Doctor grows poor. He too would have found a $1.25 fine, or its British equivalent, stiff.

In these books, parents and children get a chance to empathize with Dolittle and admire his dogged altruism. They get to act silly and speak in animals' voices—in the way people talk to and for their pets. They get to go to Africa and the South Pacific, and to travel with a circus. It's a tradition of adventure. A tradition that goes back to World War I.

Hugh Lofting, author of the Dr. Dolittle series, was stationed in the trenches. Depressed, lonely, missing his family, Lofting began to write stories home to his children, illustrated with charming drawings of the pudgy Doctor and his friends. Right from the start, the books straddled two worlds: the blood and death of the trenches; the cozy circle of the household hearth. Before the war, Lofting had been a civil engineer, traveling to places that provided locales for some of Dolittle's adventures, among them Lagos, Cuba, and Jamaica. When Lofting was invalided in the war, he was shipped home to the United States, where he lived for most of his adult life—a surprising fact, given the nineteenth-century English ambiance of the Dolittle series. After the war, the stories were expanded and printed as books, the first in 1920. By 1928 Lofting tired of the series. He sent Dr. Dolittle to the moon, hoping to be rid of him, but was pressured into publishing more volumes during the thirties and forties that are different in tone and have not been reprinted.[1]

Until the Dell edition, the tradition of reading Dr. Dolittle had lapsed in the United States from the early seventies to the late eighties after New York librarian Isabelle Suhl charged in a 1968 Bulletin of Interracial Books for Children that the Doctor "is in essence the personification of The Great White Father" and Lofting thoroughly "racist and chauvinist."[2] The books, which had undergone some localized editing of racial slurs in the 1940s, went out of print entirely in the U.S. for the first time since the twenties. Although they had always been loved for their altruism and goodwill, the books were now accused of propounding the worst kinds of prejudice and bad feelings. Ironically, Dolittle the series stood accused of precisely the kinds of ugly hierarchical thinking that Dolittle the character tries to escape. The charges stuck. When it was released in December 1967, the film version directed by Richard Fleischer and starring Rex Harrison was supposed to make Dolittle a mini-industry—with toys and dolls and a ride at Disneyworld. But after Suhl's charges got press coverage, some corporations dropped their options.[3]

In the late eighties, in time for the centenary of Lofting's birth, Dell decided to try broader editing and enlisted Lofting's relatives for the task. It added to the series an afterword written by Christopher Lofting, the author's son, pointing out that although "on principle one can make a strong argument that one should not tamper with the classics . . . times have changed." Accordingly, offensive references to racial minorities, including certain drawings and paragraphs, were deleted so that "future generations of children" could share "the opportunity to read the Doctor Dolittle stories." The decisive factor was "the strong belief that the author himself would have immediately approved making the alterations."[4]

Like many adults, I originally read the Dr. Dolittle stories in childhood. Back then, I did not perceive their racism or sexism; I simply adored the Doctor. An acquaintance and colleague who is an African Prince tuned right in when I mentioned Dr. Dolittle; he too did not remember the books as racist and had loved them as a child. I loved Dr. Dolittle so thoroughly that I sought out *The Story of Dr. Dolittle* in used bookstores towards the end of 1987, as my older daughter turned seven; I secured a 1948 edition and began to read it aloud. After 1988, I was able to finish the reading and purchase the books in the Dell edition, available at my supermarket checkout counter. I have thus had what is now the unusual experience of reading to my children a substantially unedited version of Volume One—in racial terms among the most offensive of the books—and then reading Volumes Two to Seven in the Dell version.

Basically, I approved Dell's changes. Most people today would choke on Polynesia's racial epithets and dislike the presentation in Volume One of Prince Bumpo as a vaudevillian Black Man. I also felt uncomfortable with portions having to do with women, portions that remain unchanged in the Dell edition because they are less obviously offensive and far less localized. Ms. Suhl was right in a way: Dell's alterations eliminated the most obviously biased passages but could not change certain effects of the whole. Yet Dell books and Dolittle fans are also right: neither "racism" nor "sexism" are finally what count about the Dolittle stories.

Ultimately, the books imagine a world in which all forms of prejudice would be meaningless, in which all that really mattered would be goodness of heart. Money would have no value in such a world. Racism and the abuse of animals would disappear along with social class and other hierarchies. Although as a parent and child I wanted to own the books, that very desire involves a certain paradox. For the books teach the pitfalls of ownership and possessions—and the good Doctor is a master at changing his life and giving things away. This is what children have always, I believe, understood about the books and made adults want to read them to children: Dr. Dolittle is a misfit, an outsider, someone who has cast off material things, someone so different from the norm that it's miraculous. Reading Dr. Dolittle allows us to exit the workaday world and to do little but reside with him outside of business as usual.

II

In *The Story of Dr. Dolittle*, Volume One in the series, the Doctor travels with his animal friends to Africa to return home a parrot, a crocodile, and a monkey who have been pining for home. They sail down the coast, looking for land that the animals find familiar and are, predictably enough, shipwrecked. The fishes warn them in time for all to escape without much danger but, once on land, Dolittle is captured by a tribe called the Jollijinki, who are stereotypical Africans. Dolittle easily tricks the Jollijinki and escapes by using his marvelous rapport with animals. This book typifies some contradictions in the Dolittle series: it hates hierarchies and yearns for a community of good hearts; but it keeps veering into situations and themes that look racist and sexist.

In the original version of 1920 and the mildly edited version from 1948, Dolittle relies on the African Prince Bumpo, who wants, more than anything else, to be white. It seems Bumpo has been reading fairy tales and believes he has awakened a white Sleeping Beauty. She wouldn't marry him when she saw he was black. Probably no princess but "some farmer's fat wife," Jip sneers. Dolittle promises Bumpo whiteness if the Prince will help him, then tricks the Prince into thinking he has been turned white permanently, when of course only paints and powders are involved. He feels bad about the deception, since Bumpo has "a good heart," and hopes that the chemicals will have a lasting effect—which seems unlikely. In the 1988 edition, Bumpo still helps the Doctor escape, but the whole motif of wanting to be turned white has been eliminated. Now, Dolittle hynotizes the Prince to secure his cooperation.

Episodes like that with Prince Bumpo present awkward questions in earlier versions that will be spared readers of the 1988 edition. How can we read to children paragraphs like these from the 1948 edition, conveniently deleted by Dell, in which Dolittle and Polynesia the parrot discuss the plan to turn Bumpo white:

> "This is all very well," said the Doctor. "But it isn't so easy to turn a black man white. You speak as though he were a dress to be redyed. It's not so simple. 'Shall the leopard change his spots, or the Ethiopian his skin,' you know?"
>
> "I don't know anything about that," said Polynesia impatiently. "But you must turn this man white."

More crudely, the 1920 edition used "coon" instead of "man," in the last sentence.

The answer, for me, when reading from the 1948 edition, was skipping the above paragraphs completely and changing other words as I read aloud—often (I later found) the very words altered in the Dell edition. Children's books, notoriously intended for bedtime when parents might want to shorten a chapter, almost always allow for such deletions and changes. I also found it helpful to note about the general action (we make these notations as we read) "well, isn't it silly that the book says Bumpo wants to be white. He should be happy looking just like he looks." With which the children agreed. Good liberal propaganda, to offset the flaws in the Dolittle series.

But readers of the Dell Centenary edition will not be spared awkward questions entirely. Even in the Dell edition, the Africans have weak judgment and silly names—the Jollijinki, the Fantippans, Prince Bumpo, and King Koko. Though all words related to race have been deleted, certain plot elements continue to depend on the idea that Africans are incompetent in the ways of the world. In *Dr. Dolittle's Post Office*, for example, Dolittle and his animals redeem a mail delivery system that Africans have been unable to run because they rely on stamps placed in boxes with no further human agency to effect delivery. In the same volume, when King Koko secures via parcel post a bicycle from Europe, he declares a national holiday—a small detail whose incongruity (like many in the Dolittle books) made my children laugh, in this instance at Koko's expense.

The deletion of color words does not automatically alter derogatory perceptions. In fact, one could argue that the omission of color words was unnecessary and improper since, in the Dell version, there are no black people in Africa. But I would in no way urge further changes or deletions. Views of other cultures as childish or irrational continue to be a standard feature of media coverage and popular lore. It is perhaps just as well that parents and children have the chance to discuss sneering attitudes early, in the comfortable contexts provided by the Dolittle stories. For the values of hierarchy always seem to intrude, sooner or later, into even the most altruistic dream; the Dolittle stories are no exception.

The books' "sexism" is harder to handle, because unlike the material about Africans it is not localized in specific words or paragraphs but embodied in the very plots. At the beginning of the series, for example, Dolittle lives with his sister, Sarah. The menage has the vaguely unwholesome aura of the brother-sister pairs in some of Dickens's novels and needs to be disrupted. Predictably, Sarah is obsessed by neatness and by the income from her brother's practice. The ever-growing menagerie of animals who flock to Dolittle's house threatens both. Dr. Dolittle grows poor: his very name conveys the disapproval Sarah vividly feels. It's them or me, Sarah says, or words to that effect—and is shocked when the Doctor chooses them. Sarah leaves, freeing the Doctor to be with his friends. But she turns up in several later volumes, with her eventual husband. And she's always a nuisance when she does—fainting, revealing Dolittle's identity when he wants to be in disguise, being embarrassed by how he's come down in the world.

With Sarah gone, the gender balance in the household is disturbed, but not for long. Dab-Dab, the duck, one of the few animals expressly gendered female, steps into the breach. She cooks and cleans, she fusses over finances, she becomes— her tag phrase in the stories—The Housekeeper. Dab-Dab is a drag. Whenever the adventures get really good—for example, when Dolittle establishes a triumphant circus, displacing the exploitative circus boss and sharing his profits with the animals—Dab-Dab wants to go home, to Puddleby. She moans when money that might take them home is spent instead (by the improvident Doctor) on a pasture for retired cab horses. She winces when the Doctor talks about establishing a similar retreat for dogs as well. My younger daughter says she feels sad every time Dab-Dab starts lamenting the loss of home.

Dab-Dab finally makes me feel bad too, only halfway into *Dr. Dolittle and the Green Canary,* when she starts to warn the Doctor that the impresario mounting a show featuring Dolittle's animals should turn over the profits to Dab-Dab immediately. I can tell right away that the impresario is going to steal the funds—as he does, perhaps a hundred pages later. It's depressing to think like Dab-Dab.

One of the plots gives gentle voice to this desire to be rid of the female—female caution, female domesticity, female sadness, female troubles. A seal in the circus has received word from other animals that her family misses her. Her husband, leader of the pack, went into a depression after his wife's capture and the group of seals is about to break up in chaos. Dolittle decides to help her escape. To do so, he must transport her overland to the ocean, where she can then swim northward to home. Most of the book is about the elaborate escape, aided and abetted by animals, including the sheriff's dogs. When the seal has trouble covering ground, she is dressed in widow's weeds and transported by coach. The other passengers complain about the smell and the "widow's" propensity for sliding down off her seat. Finally, they reach the water and the doctor tosses her in. Making the motif of woman-ridding explicit, he is charged with the murder of the "widow" by a passerby. There is a trial, but Dolittle gets released when a male magistrate who knows the Doctor believes his story, agreeing along the way to wink at the "theft" of the circus owner's seal. The novels contain lots of little parables of this kind about how women mess things up but also—a counternarrative—about how the family structure typical of humans is present even among animals.

The books also contain lots of digs against capitalism and private property—as when the magistrate agrees to overlook the theft of the seal. In fact, some of the stories skirt the genre of Orwell's *Animal Farm,* which uses animals to make points about flaws in human society. Returning home from the war, Lofting would have stepped into a world undergoing fundamental changes. He would have found, for example, active labor movements that raised new questions about management and labor. The novels participate in the social dialogue about changes in class and labor structures. They protest the exploitation of workers (represented here by the cab horses and the circus folk) and prefer socialism or, at least, enlightened profit-sharing or employee ownership of firms. In *Doctor Dolittle's Circus,* for example, Dolittle provokes a corrupt circus manager to desert his troupe. He then builds the circus into a fabulously successful unit by giving each of the circus's acts a share of the ownership and a part of the profits. In another striking episode, from *Dr. Dolittle's Caravan,* Dr. Dolittle negotiates a contract for his dog, Jip, by which the animal receives part of the profits from the sale of an item he endorses in advertisements.

The books conform to children's notions of justice or, to use their own term, "what's fair or unfair." That may be part of the pleasure in reading them as an adult, years after it has become clear that the world is often an unfair place. The books present a blend of capitalism and socialism, at a distance, in the distant, vaguely Victorian fictional landscape of Dolittle's England. It's a magical world, in which humans and animals unite.

In literature intended for children, girls and boys (especially peasant boys) often have a magical rapport with animals: Mary in *The Secret Garden,* with her robin friend and then Colin and Dickon (the peasant lad who also talks to animals); the girl in *Black Beauty* or the one in *Island of the Blue Dolphins;* Fern in *Charlotte's Web,* until puberty, when she inexplicably becomes more interested in the boy next door. It is quite common for animals to appear as people, in plots that dramatize moral situations or the facts of everyday life: Aesop's *Fables,* the Sweet Pickles books, the Berenstain Bears. Children adore these books, and year after year, generation after generation, parents—usually mothers—read them aloud to their children. The stories bridge animal and human, child and adult worlds. The readings may bespeak the desire for such bridging in the years after childhood.

The Dolittle books' fundamental instinct, an instinct children have always understood, is that the man-woman-child family structure—like the belief that certain people are inferior to others—is part and parcel of a world in which humans relate to animals and to money in ways different from Dolittle's. It's a competitive and hurtful world, epitomized by the name given one of Dolittle's animals, the pushmi-pullyu: Push-Me, Pull-You. The Dolittle stories are designed to explore—creatively and gently, in a nonthreatening way—

alternatives to all of that. They are also, contradictorily, meant to be read to children within the nuclear household itself, and to be purchased by middle-class parents for their children.

For Doctor Dolittle, devotion to animals is a crossroads. To live with animals means growing poor and living apart from human society. He reminds me in this sense of other fictional characters who are torn between the animal and human worlds, the "natural" and the "civilized": Tarzan, for example, raised by apes but married to domestic Jane; or Mowgli in *The Jungle Book,* fostered by wolves but banished in adolescence to a human village. He reminds me too of actual figures like Dian Fossey, whose devotion to gorillas led, seemingly inexorably, to a misanthropic distance from almost everyone who knew her and probably provoked, one dark night, her brutal murder.

For us who read about figures like Dolittle or Tarzan or Fossey, the commitment to animals does not imply a similar breach. We don't have to choose between animals and human society, in part because the animals—for those of us who only read about them—are not real. Someone like Fossey perceived animals as of paramount concern—and felt compelled to act in ways that worked against economic success, good health, ordinary happiness. When we read Dolittle we understand him to be, within the confines of a children's narrative, a charming eccentric. A similar devotion to animals might not wear well in a neighbor, say, or in someone who policed our dietary habits. For most of us, the fair treatment of animals is an admirable goal, for which we work selectively rather than with every fiber in our being. That, we tell ourselves, is the difference between living a liberal, humane life and a fanatical one. When they are read in children's rooms, the Dolittle books allow for the acquisitive life, even as they question some of its values.

III

When I was a child living in a small apartment, I never had a serious pet—just guppies one year and then a parakeet, named Dicky. Dicky was an okay bird, though kind of dull. After a few years, we ceased to notice him, until he became the victim of my mother's clean floors. Every spring, she would launch a ferocious attack on all the dirt in the house, there being, in reality, not much. One year this process included using a mixture of ammonia and bleach on the wood floors. She kept the windows wide open but the next day there was Dicky—feet up at the bottom of his cage.

Until I was an adult, I never had another pet. But I began to surround myself with pictures of animals, though not photographs of cute kittens or any of the usual stuff. The first print I purchased was of the Bison from the Altamira caves— the animal huge, springing powerfully from one end of the print to the other, captured by some prehistoric artist in mid-flight. The first one I had framed was of the unicorn tapestry: the white unicorn hemmed in by a white fence, on a field of green spotted by symbolic flowers. It's significant that these are not photos of animals—but stylized representations of them. It is also significant that the animals themselves are symbolic—the unicorn of Christ or, if you will, of a mythical, magical beast with healing powers, a female animal possessing a phallic horn; the bison of the social unity and fertility of the prehistoric hunt. In the Dolittle series, animals are also symbolic. Dolittle's devotion to the animals signifies his being outside the usual values of his community and in touch with something else: goodness, nature, psychic health—spiritual but not material power. I've compared him to Tarzan and Fossey—and those are apt comparisons. But the best comparison of all is with St. Francis of Assisi—the gentle friend of the poor and of animals, surrounded in legend and in images of him by chattering larks.

Like Dolittle, St. Francis was someone of good family who chucked it all to devote himself to the needy—in his case, needy lepers, rather than animals. He was the son of a wealthy merchant whose Papa expected him to keep up the family business and was shocked when Francis took instead to stripping off his clothes to symbolize his devotion to the Lady Poverty and spent all his time nursing the poor. Papa saw poverty as a stigma and shame—and his son's embrace of poverty as a sign of madness. He disowned his son.[5]

But to Francis poverty was not a problem but the natural condition of the spiritual life. Poverty made him free. Francis was not someone sad or dreary, but full of life and the spirit of adventure. Someone who in the darkest hours of his life (when the Church tried to force him to follow rules and acquire possessions) would compose and sing a song of the joy of nature. Someone who just couldn't see or recognize as valid what the "real" world kept demanding of him.[6] Someone sane who acted like a madman; someone smart who acted like a simpleton. A holy man. Someone who leads and makes you want to follow—even if, as usually happens, you don't.[7]

I felt the attraction to Dolittle and his animals very strongly. I connect it with certain people I have known, like my friend Dick Chernick (in "Crossing Ocean Parkway"), who gave up teaching and a middle-class life for a shack shared with animals in rural New Jersey. The source of the attraction remains, and probably must remain, misty. But I want to end with a story, a memory, that makes it a little clearer.

AROUND THE CORNER FROM MY parents' apartment, for the years and years of my youth, was a tiny, and slightly dingy, candy store. Off the beaten track, just a few blocks from much grander stores, this candy store was still the ultimate resource for me until the age of ten. I remember one summer night, after dinner, cruising to the store and seeing in the window an object that transfixed my desires. It was a ceramic piggy bank, but with a felt covering that made it look more like a plush toy: a chubby, pink-orange pig that I remember now as looking like Wilbur in the animated version of *Charlotte's Web.*

It wasn't the functional value of the pig that transfixed me—I hardly perceived it as a bank at all. Nor was it really a tie, a direct tie, to animals. It was the plushness and pigginess of the thing, its sheer adorableness that made me want to own it. But it wasn't a purely acquisitive feeling either. Rather, as in the stories about Dolittle, Tarzan, Fossey, and St. Francis, the pig represented feelings that sound too grand when they are put into words. The animal-like thing—in this case the plush surfaced pig—provides a satisfaction in between the material and the natural. It symbolizes solidarity with the natural world. Yet it also belongs to the material world—is in fact something on sale at the local store.

Other forms of ownership—of sweaters or bikes, for example—wouldn't be the same. Having the animal, or the representation of the animal, was purer than that, more complicated than that. The pig represented a wholeness: nature humanized, brought into the home, accessible in symbolic form at a glance. A reminder of nature as we like to think it existed in states of mind before modernity, a magical state of wholeness between the human and the not-human that may never have existed but that exerts a powerful hold on the imagination.

I yearned for that pig, counted pennies, but simply didn't have enough. For maybe a week or ten days, the pig stood in the window, and I planned to buy it. And then it was gone, and its duplicate never appeared. But the feeling remained, ready to be reanimated by the effect that books about figures like Dr. Dolittle have on people like me.

Notes

1. Not much has been published about Lofting. These facts come from *Longman Companion to Twentieth-Century Literature,* ed. A. C. Ward, rev. by Margaret Hussey, 3rd ed. (New York: Longman, 1981), 321; *Authors of Books for Young People* (Metuchen, N.J.: Scarecrow Press, 1971), 322; and Edward Blishen, *Hugh Lofting* (London: Bodley Head, 1968).

2. Accounts of the controversy about the Dolittle books appear in Maureen O'Brien, "Dr. Dolittle Is Back: In Carefully Revised Editions for Today's Readers," *Publisher's Weekly* (February 26, 1968), 122; and Selma G. Lanes, "Doctor Doolittle [*sic*]: Innocent Again," *New York Times Book Review* (August 28, 1988), 20. Suhl is quoted in Lanes's essay.

3. Suhl's charges probably marred the success of the movie and of a planned Dolittle industry equivalent to that surrounding Mickey Mouse; see the high hopes expressed in "The Dolittle Explosion," *Newsweek* 71 (January 1, 1968), 58.

4. The full afterword appears at the end of the Dolittle books in the Dell Yearling edition.

5. For Francis's biography, see A. M. Almedingen, *Francis of Assisi: A Portrait* (London: Bodley Head, 1967) and Anthony Mockler, *Francis of Assisi: The Wandering Years* (New York: Dutton, 1976).

6. Almost from the beginning of Francis's mission, the Catholic Church wanted to annex and change it, especially its vow of complete poverty. The Church eventually succeeded, by exploiting rifts among his followers when Francis was on pilgrimage to the Holy Land. Francis was broken and sad to learn that many of his "little brothers" never did understand the spirit of his movement, but his greatest triumph was still ahead—the vision on Monte Verde, where he is said to have received the stigmata.

7. One of Francis's radical contributions was what is called the Tertiary Order—a collection of people who continued to marry and live in the world, under modified vows of poverty, but who accepted Francis's rule in spirit.

S i x

The Paglia Principle

I

For every admirer of Camille Paglia, there is someone stunned into silence by the flood of her rhetoric and someone else who feels rabid fury. An exhibitionist they say, a vaudevillian, a clown, a traitor. They say, you notice she never taught anywhere good after Bennington—and she never will. Or they say nothing at all, rolling their eyes back in exasperation at the very mention of her name.

I've been suspicious of Paglia ever since I first heard about her—a female Italian American professor, author of *Sexual Personae,* making a career out of bad-mouthing feminism and talking about how academics today are dullards, frauds, or worse. I've had a grudge against her ever since I saw her on the cover of *New York* magazine. Then I got to see her everywhere: *Harper's,* the *New York Times Book Review,* the *New Republic, People, Playboy, Cosmopolitan, New Woman, Vanity Fair.* So I thought I'd settle into a nice, juicy, exposé of Paglia— close to my heart, and useful since she's still getting so much attention. Imagine my surprise when I read *Sexual Personae* and discovered all that I expected—but much more.

SEXUAL PERSONAE HAS SOLD A LOT of copies, but it's hard to believe that very many people have read it from end to end, or even in considerable sections. The book is a full-blooded account of art and decadence that claims that art arises from a fear of primal chaos, with chaos equivalent, in Paglia's view, to femaleness. In a Nietzschean mode, *Sexual Personae* claims that Western art originates in Apollonian flight from nature as Dionysian, chthonic principle, voraciously sucking everything into a vortex of dissolution. What complicates the picture, according to Paglia, is that art always veers into sexual personae and hence into decadence, a kind of parodic, camped-up version of the devouring female principle that it wanted to avoid. With its taste for the flamboyant, the book is like a demonic Ariel and Will Durant's history of the West compressed into one very long volume. It's like Gibbon's *The Decline and Fall of the Roman Empire*—a flashy, stylistic tour de force with a passion for "the decline."

The book moves from prehistory to Egypt, to Greece, to Rome, to the Renaissance, to eighteenth-century Gothic. More than half covers the nineteenth century, with chapters on just about every major writer and artist in England, the U.S., and the Continent. The book makes some nasty comments about academics and feminists. One of Paglia's best-known maxims, for example, is: "If civilization had been left in female hands, we would still be living in grass huts." Sensational quips like that have received almost all the attention. But Paglia really means for *Sexual Personae* to be a history of Western art and sensibility viewed through images of sexuality that haunt the human imagination—the sexual personae of the title.

Paglia's favorite personae are the *kouros*, the beautiful boy, slim and girlish in form but with masculine genitals that become the focal point of male sexual desire, and the Egyptian god Khepera, an *uroboros*, circular, serpentlike, able to reach tongue to tail, and remarkable, says Paglia, for masturbatory pleasure. Lots of Paglia's favorite sexual personae are androgynous or homosexual. In fact, when she is not saying crude and outlandish things about male homosexuals—as she often does—Paglia believes they are responsible for most of what is notable in Western civilization. She shows no similar preference for female homosexuals, who, like almost all the female sexual personae, Paglia regards with distaste or displeasure. The exceptions, in *Sexual Personae*, are the Amazon and the virago—types Paglia admires, and indeed lives.

Now I pride myself on having a wide range of subjects I know, teach, and write about. But I've got to admit it: I would never think of writing an encyclopedic book like *Sexual Personae*. I envy its ambition and possible existence as a quirky and cranky classic. But it's not, finally, a book I would want to have written. I agree, absolutely, with the gist of most reviews. This is an amazing book, written in a provocative style that sometimes makes you laugh out loud with pleasure. It is also an infuriating, difficult, obsessive, and in some ways crazy book. I really do think it could become a classic—but a classic of a certain sort, because Paglia is a certain kind of critic. An excessive critic, a self-destructive critic, a critic who has a few brilliant ideas (with variations), but maybe nothing more. A critic who might not develop or might become a universal joke—or might turn out to be for the ages. If she's very, very lucky, she will be like Nietzsche, one of her sources—frequently cited, much less frequently read, everybody's idea of an astonishing thinker, but someone in danger of ending up mad. If she's unlucky, she will be more like Christopher Smart. And if you don't know who he is, that says it all.

Paglia's most consistent lament is that she was neglected as a critic and scholar for twenty years— "twenty years! twenty

years!" like Catherine Earnshaw's ghost in *Wuthering Heights.*
After a Yale Ph.D. and a stint at Bennington, she dropped off
the academic map into a job at the University of the Arts in
Philadelphia. I visited there in 1990. It's a lively and stimulat-
ing place that doesn't deserve to be off the academic map,
though it's nothing like Harvard, Yale, or even N.Y.U. or Tem-
ple. It's an arts school and the students are artsy.

The night I lectured there, about forty people lingered for
almost an hour after the formal question period ended—even
though it was already after 10 P.M. The place was just getting
revved up around midnight. When most universities are dark
and quiet, University of the Arts students are coming and
going on the way to their studios. People sat around drinking
wine and shooting the bull. That night we moved from talking
about body piercing to talking about Frida Kahlo (the sensational woman artist who did self-portraits during her marriage
to Mexican artist Diego Rivera) and Madonna (who owns a
collection of Kahlo). How both women pose and vamp for the
audience, one sculptor said; but how they torture their bodies
to create the image of glamor and allure. I heard about Kahlo's
mutilated body, wrecked in an automobile accident; about
Madonna's arduous bodybuilding routines. This kind of connection between body piercing, Kahlo's art, and Madonna's
self-absorption is the kind of connection that gets made at the
University of the Arts—and it's the kind of connection Paglia
loves. I was cruising through this territory as an interested
observer and enjoying it. I couldn't help thinking, Gee, I had
forgotten how different arts people are from English professors.

Paglia is an English professor who is like an arts person. She
probably keeps irregular hours and eats lousy food. She loves
to make bold generalizations and comparisons, some of which
actually work. She certainly allows herself to act up in public,
often adopting one of the sexual personae that form the loose

thesis of her book. *People* posed her as a gang member and streetfighter—tough and butch, in jeans, a jacket, brushed back hair, acne-shadowed face, switchblade open menacingly in her hand. At the end of the article, they showed her in her classroom, wearing a classic sheath and a demure string of pearls, looking as though she ran a finishing school for the hip-looking kids who surrounded her. Other photo-ops have shown her as Joan of Arc, Napoleon, and Hamlet (the last two were roles Paglia chose, as a child, at Halloween). She's an exhibitionist all right, and unlike other exhibitionists in academia, her hunger for publicity moves way beyond the standard poses in front of bookcases, desks, or grassy campus knolls.

It's unusual that someone as well known as Paglia should be at the University of the Arts, for years as associate, not full, professor. But it's not at all unusual that Paglia had a low-profile career before *Sexual Personae*. In simple terms, academics have to publish what their home institutions expect them to publish. "Publish or perish" is an accurate statement—but far more variable than it seems to people outside colleges and universities. Some institutions do require a book, or even two books, before tenure. But many colleges and universities, even most, require only a few articles that they agree to accept as a gesture towards future work—if they like you well enough. Before *Sexual Personae*, Paglia had published nothing significant. More important, she does not seem to have made people like her, except for her powerful mentor, Harold Bloom. She paid the price, but also preserved her spirit during her twenty years far from the limelight. What attracts people to Paglia is that she does not have the lackluster, sad-sack quality of many professors. In fact, a high-pitched attack mode is the essence of the Paglia principle.

When I was thinking of taking my first job at a small elite college, I remember talking with a graduate professor I much admired who was a really excellent teacher. Like many professors, he had published only one book, an expanded version of his dissertation, many years before. "If you go to that college," he said, "you can be a big fish in a little pond." "That might be good. We have only one idea," he said, "and your dissertation [on epilogues in novels] was probably yours." His remarks sent goosebumps of fear up my back, even though I was much less than certain at the time that I had even one good idea. This was the same kind of talk I heard all the time at the small college, which, despite its elitism, represents attitudes towards publication typical of nonresearch, teaching institutions: publish "one stunning article," be like Henry James, with "a mind so fine that no idea could violate it," work on "your book" (always singular) to get it right for years and years (twenty years was the usual figure).

Paglia—it turns out—was nestled at Bennington during the years I was at this small college in New England. She did not play it safe by producing a few articles, maybe even a book, on the way to the Big Book and being, in general, a good girl. I don't know whether she was reading, obsessing, and thinking about *Sexual Personae* (I rather suspect she was) but she didn't do more manageable tasks in the meantime. Much worse, I suspect, was that she was considered disorderly at Bennington (at Bennington! not known for its decorum) and is reported to have gotten into a fistfight that led to her arranged departure.

Sexual Personae was a long time a-coming and, unless you acquire the general reputation of being "smart" in academia, you can't get away with that. And "smart" usually goes along with being male and good-looking in a way that men think is good-looking. "Smart" is usually a word used in male-bonding, academic style. One friend says (and I think she's right, at least for heterosexuals) that it has to do with who got to take the prettiest girl to the senior prom. It's hard for women to be "smart" in academia without really trying, and the essence of qualities that provoke the adjective is NOT trying—but being a kind of cross between (sexual personae) Adonis and Apollo. In fact, as it turns out, *Sexual Personae* is not a "smart" book— no one would ever take it to the senior prom. But it is a brilliant one—scintillating, hot, streaked with weird but sometimes wonderful insights—but uneven, overall.

Because it's always high-pitched and on the attack, always opting for maximum shock value, *Sexual Personae* has some serious flaws. Paglia tends to repeat herself and certain themes—such as the lesbian vampire—crop up everywhere. She leans heavily to one side of any interpretation—so that when Emily Dickinson refers to a "cloven brain," it has to be axe-murderer stuff and not a metaphor for psychic pain. (I can imagine Paglia's response: Only a bullshit professor would care about psychic pain! Axe murders are what make civilization great!) Paglia has a penchant for saying critics have ignored certain topics when they have discussed them a great deal (one example: Emily Brontë's Heathcliff as a masculine projection of Brontë's own Byronic nature). To balance this neglect of prior critics, Paglia sometimes raves and rants against silly, but minor, interpretations (like one critic's identification of Heathcliff with Emily's ineffectual brother, Branwell).

Paglia uses straw men all the time and does not seem to know about critics others find important. She does not conform to the usual scholarly standards. I'm not overly bothered by that, since so many people do meet those standards with less interesting results. But I am bothered that, in her many interviews, so dogmatic a nonconformist as Paglia seems outraged when she is not rewarded or praised by the academic establishment. Is she still waiting to be taken to the senior prom?

Paglia makes much of being Italian American and portrays herself as a tough, working-class street kid. She accuses other academics of hiding their ethnicity, of trying to please the WASP establishment.[1] But Paglia's father was a college professor and the family was central Italian—both unusual, not typical, of Italian Americans. There's a lot of willful downward mobility in Paglia, a lot of slumming. Italian Americans have a code for it: Paglia is a central Italian who wants to be "a Sicilian." At the same time, she courts certain portions of WASP-dom. Conservative male critics love her: after all, she states their own prejudices so colorfully. Paglia feels thrilled that she has lectured at M.I.T. and been mentioned in *The Harvard Crimson*. She even reprints the lecture *and the entire question period* (this, I believe, a first) in *Sex, Art, and American Culture*, which lists the *Crimson* notice as an "article" about Paglia.

Paglia's an odd bird and *Sexual Personae* maps her oddness. I want to get at her obsessions through sentences flagged by Paglia in her heavy-handed way ("I said," "I say," "My thesis") as crucial to her argument:

> Male bonding and patriarchy were the recourse to which man was forced by his terrible sense of woman's power, her imperviousness, her archetypal confederacy with chthonian nature. . . . The historical repugnance to woman has a rational basis: disgust is reason's proper response to the grossness of procreative nature.

> Personality is architectonic. Without virile force, the self slips back into the dissolution of swampy female nature.[2]

Typical readers may be confused by these amorphous sentences and their references to abstractions. Yet the remarks really do take us to the heart of Paglia's argument. Very much like Freud, Paglia associates masculinity ("virile force") with the individual, art, and social order. What "virile force" must and should control is dissolution, chaos, impersonal nature—all associated by Paglia axiomatically (if not logically) with the "swampy female."

What needs to be said, and in no uncertain terms, is that *Sexual Personae* is a book filled with fear, hatred, and loathing of the female body: heterosexual and lesbian. Paglia's appeal is that she is a woman saying all this about females—the same stuff some men have been saying for years—Nietzsche's own "stinking pudenda" in the mouth of a woman who claims to be a feminist.

In fact, Paglia makes a good case against women, all the more convincing for being made by a woman who calls herself a feminist and cites some female sources with approval, even if she distorts what they say (I am thinking here of how Paglia praises but misrepresents Jane Harrison, who saw Greece as a "primitive" Dionysian culture).[3] But once you see how Paglia hates female bodies, and on what basis, the case—not to mention Paglia's theses—begins to fall apart. I want to talk about Camille Paglia and the female body.

II

I hate what Camille Paglia has to say about women. I don't believe most of it is accurate or anything like the whole story. Here is some of what she says, for example, about menstruation, which for Paglia is the major activity of female life:

> Menstrual blood is the stain, the birthmark of original sin, the filth that transcendental religion must wash from man. Is this identification merely phobic, merely misogynistic? Or is it possible there is something uncanny about menstrual blood, justifying its attachment to taboo? (11)

Paglia knows that hatred of women is often based on fear of the mother who looms large in childhood—the authority figure, potent, overwhelming, and dangerous. This fear explains the clever identification of womb and tomb, a perennial favorite in the misogynistic hit parade: born of the mother, man is always in danger of domination by the mother, absorption by her to the point of nonbeing. This is one reason Freud

associated women with narcissism, and with a regressive fore-
taste of death. But, as you probably sense from the above passage, Paglia is about to rescue fear of women from charges that
it is "merely" phobic and misogynistic by showing that to her
it makes good sense. She's going to trot out that tune in a different key:

> I will argue that it is not menstrual blood per se which dis-
> turbs the imagination—unstaunchable as that red flood might
> be—but rather the albumen in the blood, the uterine shreds,
> placental jellyfish of the female sea. This is the chthonian
> matrix from which we rose. We have an evolutionary revul-
> sion from slime, our site of biologic origins.(11)

A student of menstrual blood, Paglia gets fixed on the globs
that sometimes (by Jove, she's right) appear on a tampon or
napkin or floating in the bowl. I never thought I would write
that sentence. But then I never thought I would find someone
for whom "placental jellyfish" (a clever image) would signify
primal flux instead of (biologically speaking) evidence of no
pregnancy that month—washing out the uterus being, after
all, what menstruation is.

Nor do things get better if menstruation ceases, in pregnancy:

> Woman's body is a sea acted upon by the month's lunar wave-
> motion. Sluggish and dormant, her fatty tissues are gorged
> with water, then suddenly cleansed at hormonal high tide.
> Edema is our mammalian relapse into the vegetable. Preg-
> nancy demonstrates the deterministic character of woman's
> sexuality. Every pregnant woman has body and self taken over
> by a chthonian force beyond her control. (11)

Paglia gives gestation a bad name. It's not a positive state at
all—none of those little flutter kicks that pregnant women love,
just throbbing to chthonian force. Given this prejudice, it's

odd—but I think significant—that Paglia scarcely mentions labor and birth. All those intense contractions in transition (the last stage of labor) and the pain and stress of pushing would seem like her element. Primal, all right, even with the Apollonian control of Lamaze breathing. But the end of the process is birth, giving birth. And that's something Paglia doesn't seem to get.

Show Paglia a newborn and she sees a blob, a tortured being, a mess of sexual personae, ultimately a corpse. Show her a male erection and she sees something threatened by the vagina dentata (which all vaginas are, "metaphorically," Paglia actually says). There's no "before" or "during" or "again" for Paglia. There's only a terrifying "after"—and that's why decadence is her subject, her only subject.

Paglia's views on pregnancy and menstruation are bizarre, but not outside the boundaries of imagination. In fact, they took me back to a moment long forgotten in which I imagined pregnancy as a dark, deadly force. When I was about twelve, my mother was talking to my cousin's wife, Ann, one of our closest relatives. Ann had two living children, and was pregnant with her third. But she had also lost two babies at birth because of the Rh-factor. Ann was talking about childbirth, the birth of her own children or someone else's. I don't remember the details. But I remember associating pregnancy with death and clenching my teeth in the living room the next day, fantasizing about my future life, as I often did at this time. I was going to be an air force captain or a journalist. It would turn out that even though I was married, I would be sterile and could never have children and would not have to undergo the dangers I had heard Ann describe. How I rued that fantasy in later life, given my complicated history of childbearing. But having had that fantasy makes it easier for me to understand Paglia.

Of course, not all women have children—some choose not

to, some can't, some don't have the chance, some have children but don't raise them, some raise children to whom they did not give birth. And no woman spends every minute of every day immersed in potential or actual pregnancy: there being, if nothing else, a life before and after the childbearing years. Despite Paglia's sense of female difference, it is scientifically true that women are no more awash in the biological flux than men are. It's just that the hormones and cycles are different. But such facts are almost beside the point—Paglia's and mine.

Never have I found it more tempting to defend menstruation, pregnancy, and birth than when reading Paglia. Menstruation may be "the Curse" for some women almost all the time and for most women some of the time. But it also can be a satisfying experience to see that blood on a tampon or pad, certifying that everything is working right on schedule. When menstruation coincides, as it often does (statistically, like the number of women in labor), with a full moon, there's a sense of something, but it's not being adrift in a primal sea. It's more like being in tune with physical, gravitational forces.

In some cultures, menstruation is a cause for celebration as well as taboo, and one can see why. There's a sign of growth, change: the potential for bearing new life. In fact, there are respected theories that see men not as fearing menstruation but yearning to imitate it—hence the penchant for initiations that involve circumcision or subcision, or other wounds. Some people think that early religions worshiped females because women have the power to give life, which is symbolized by menstruation. So while Paglia accents these things darkly—it's all chthonic horror, and revulsion—they can be, and have been, accented very differently. She is right, of course, that some great writers (Emily Brontë, for example) share her grim view of female bodies, menstruation, and birth. But such views are hardly a criterion for greatness: for her, a leading criterion.

Paglia talks about heading a movement called Pagan Italian Catholicism but, on the evidence of *Sexual Personae* and her many interviews, this is something she could never do. For one thing, she's a solo act, a consummate individualist, with no feeling for community or leadership at all. For another, she lacks at least half the spirit that would have to inform Pagan Italian Catholicism. Paglia says that, in church, she used to focus on a statue of St. Sebastian and on another of St. Lucy, offering her eyes on a platter.[4] Paglia probably also liked the Stations of the Cross and the Agnus Dei—with the whole congregation abased and beating its chest before the Lamb of God.

I liked the Wedding at Cana, the tongues of fire, and a few other zippy Gospel readings. And I loved the elevation of the host prior to communion—the bells and the mumbling in Latin, all the better when accompanied by wafts of incense— the movement towards the sublime and miraculous. Although I am a distinctly lapsed Catholic, I still have the crosses I used to wear and a "Sacred Heart of Jesus" pocket mirror my mother got from a funeral home and left in a pocketbook she borrowed from me: a feminine-looking Jesus vamping at the viewer while offering his anatomically correct heart. It seemed like sacrilege to throw them in the trash and so I stashed them in the back of a bureau drawer. Despite my superstitious veneration, I would never propose myself as the leader of Pagan Italian anything. I'd also never follow Paglia. She doesn't have a feel for spirit and sublimity—part of any decent paganism, as is a feeling for Mary as a transmuted goddess. As a leader of Italian Pagan Catholicism, Paglia is all mouth and no substance. She is hollow at the core, and the hollowness started, I think, very early, in her relationship to being female—in combination with her take on being Italian American.

III

I think Camille Paglia has internalized the way that Italian Americans are trained to think about women. She says that if sex change operations had been available when she was an adolescent, she might have had one—and I can see that in almost everything written by or about her.[5] I see it too in the way that Paglia unambiguously admires her ethnic origins. I think Paglia long ago identified with the Italian American male sense that women can be good, but men are always better. It's usually the sons who get idolized in typical Italian American homes; the daughters usually feel left out and resentful. But Paglia has mastered typical Italian American male patterns: she's tough, she's brusque, and when someone challenges or annoys her, she tries to intimidate by flying into a raving, potentially violent rage. I've seen many Italian males act this way, but never a woman. In part, Paglia idealizes Italian Americans because she has toyed with the idea that she is a man trapped in a female body. For her the womb may be the tomb of a possible, and preferred, self.

Profiles of Paglia say that she has been a lesbian but is now bisexual, but also that she rarely has affairs of any kind.[6] I can see that too. Her praise for the *uroboros* is, like everything about her, indiscreet. I was glad that she made this information public, though, because I think it's important in understanding her. I need to be clear here: I am not aware of harboring any prejudice against lesbians or bisexuals; to me these are private matters and options as good as any other. In fact, I see Paglia's lesbianism/bisexuality as part of a more basic impulse: the bad-girl impulse, which for Italian American women can take different forms. Sometimes it takes the form I took—showing professional drive that is valued only for men, not for women, but conforming in other ways. Sometimes it takes the form Madonna parodies—the vamp/tramp thumbing the nose at expectations of chastity outside marriage and coming to "no good." Paglia chose variations on both these roles: she did well in school and chose a profession but refused to do what the profession expected of her. More, she refused to do what any Italian girl should—marry and have children. She took things further by announcing publicly her lesbianism and bisexuality—and in *People* magazine, no less.

Paglia's a bad girl gone wild, a bad girl to the nth degree. But life has handed her a surprise. *Sexual Personae* came out at a time of reaction against feminism and literary theory—at the height of the debate about "political correctness." She's the same bad girl she was at Bennington, but now the establishment has a use for her. Because her badness takes the form of denigrating women and ridiculing literary theory, she is reaping social benefits instead of disapproval.

Paglia relishes—absolutely relishes—all the attention she's getting, especially since she still gets to play the bad girl, the rebel, thumbing her nose at the evil feminists and deconstructionists. She's got what all bad girls crave: recognition and success, but accompanied by the proper amount of resistance. Still, when I read Paglia or listen to her, I sense a deep unhappiness at the core. Although she comes from a family in which the father was a college professor, Paglia's experience has the true Italian American touch—so maybe I can judge. Her father's name was Pasquale; my father's name was Salvatore. I hated Marianna as a name when I was small, Americanizing its pronunciation into the wimpy Mary Ann. I would have hated a name like Camille even more—an old lady's name, smelling of funeral parlors, black dresses, withered skin: "Figlia, figlia mia, baciami." No thanks.

What would it have been like for a Camille Paglia to grow up in an Italian American household? I can only imagine from my own experience. When I was growing up, my parents always compared me invidiously to two of my cousins—the

prettier, more feminine and domestic Gina and the more popular Danielle. Ironically, neither was a blood relative: Gina
was adopted; Danielle was the daughter of my parents' best
man and maid of honor (their "goom-ba") and only honorifi-
cally called cousin. Why can't you cook like cousin Gina? Why
can't you have more friends like cousin Danielle? were regular
litanies in my life. I suspect similar comparisons were made in
Paglia's family and that her Halloween stints as Napoleon and
Hamlet drew forth dark predictions from her aunts and neighbors—all of which (as is their wont) came true.

My blond, blue-eyed cousin Gina always played "what will
it be like when we are married" games. We would spend hours
planning our husbands' names and hair color; what we would
name sons and daughters; even the color of the master bedroom. Danielle played Monopoly almost obsessively, and word
games. She played 45s on her Victrola—a corny collection featuring Teresa Brewer's "Jinglebell Rock" and other classics. I
stopped being unfavorably compared to Gina only a few years
ago. But I stopped being compared to Danielle, mysteriously,
when I was about thirteen and she was about sixteen. Like me
as a kid, Danielle was dark, tall, and big-boned. But when I
stopped growing at five feet, five inches, Danielle kept going
until she was almost a strapping six feet.

One day my parents asked me to be "careful" when I was
alone with Danielle and to let them know if anything "funny"
happened. When I asked what they meant, they muttered
something about Danielle being a little "strange" and just
urged me not to be alone with her, especially in bedrooms.
Danielle was known to sleepwalk, and at first I thought that
was the problem—that she might fall asleep and sleepwalk and
that would scare me, or she could turn violent. Then I began
to notice that Danielle's voice was very deep, and so were some
of her friends'. Her hair was short, like mine, but real short—
and she didn't style and tease it the way I did. She had little

hairs above her lip, like most brunettes, but more than most. Her friends grabbed each other around the shoulders and patted each other's behinds—like men do during a basketball game. You get the idea. I got the idea eventually. Danielle was a lesbian, who has now lived with a female partner for many years. Neither Danielle nor any of her friends ever did anything "strange" towards me and I stopped hanging around with them once the three-year gap between our ages began to seem unbridgeable in high school. Danielle's father, my Uncle Vinny, was the first of my parents' friends to die, suddenly, one night, of a heart attack. "It killed him," my father said. "It broke his heart." The news about Danielle.

Now Paglia's father is a college professor and Uncle Vinny ran an elevator—which suggests a big gap in education, worldliness, and attitudes towards homosexuals. I am not advancing Italian Americans' rigid enforcement of sex roles as iron-clad proof about Paglia's adolescence or anything else. Nor am I insisting on a one-to-one comparison between Paglia and my cousin, although Paglia, it must be said, looks like a smaller, thinner version of Danielle. Rather, it's that I suspect Paglia has had a tough row to hoe, in part from the way she hoes it now with a vengeance.

I feel sorry for Paglia, not because she is a lesbian or a bisexual and not because she teaches at the University of the Arts. I feel sorry for Paglia because she hates female bodies and denigrates almost every form of female sexuality. She is letting herself be used by people who like to hear her talk about it. She's getting a lot out of it—fame, lecture fees, book contracts—hey, I'd love to be on the cover of *New York* magazine. But she's almost out of control, and it's scary to watch her veer into action.

After twenty years of ignoring her, people are listening to Camille Paglia. She can't stop talking. *Sexual Personae* is a long (700-page) and uneven book. She could have cut repetitions and still written an enviable blockbuster. Her second book, *Sex, Art, and American Culture,* was published two years after *Sexual Personae* and was clearly intended to cash in on her notoriety. It is too trivial to be called a collection of essays, containing, as it does, op-ed columns, book reviews, and other Camille Paglia memorabilia. *Sex, Art, and American Culture* is an embarrassing bore that sold amazingly well but still bodes ill for the announced sequel to *Sexual Personae.* This sequel will cover twentieth-century pop culture—which already forms a constant point of reference in her first two books. I suspect that Paglia is going to be true to her past in ways she does not even suspect yet: that she's going to end up disappointing and alienating everyone, including her current backers; that she's going to self-destruct. Paglia may surprise me—she's done it before. But I'm afraid she'll keep talking when she has nothing more to say. And I don't think she will have more to say until she dives into the source of her own associations and judgments and figures out why she loves and hates what she does. And she does, this woman, love and hate.

Notes

1. Camille Paglia, *Sex, Art, and American Culture: Essays* (New York: Vintage, 1992), 255.

2. Camille Paglia, *Sexual Personae* (New York: Vintage, 1991), 12, 294. Originally published by Yale University Press, 1990.

3. Among Jane Harrison's books are *Prolegomena to the Study of Greek Religion* (London: Merlin Press, 1962), *Ancient Art and Ritual* (London: Thorton Butterworth, 1913), and *Mythology* (Boston: Marshall Jones, 1924).

4. See Francesca Stanfill, "Woman Warrior: Sexual Philosopher Camille Paglia Jousts with the Politically Correct," *New York* 24, no. 9 (March 4, 1991), 26; and *Sexual Personae,* 630.

5. *Sex, Art, and American Culture,* 256.

6. See Paula Chin, "Street Fighting Woman: Academic Brawler Camille Paglia Takes on the Campus Establishment," *People* 37 (April 20, 1992), 125–26+.

S e v e n

The Godfather as the World's Most Typical Novel

When I wrote about The Godfather in 1986, I slipped in references to Italian Americans and felt as though I had put chocolate kisses inside my critical essay—little autobiographical nuggets, pieces of myself. This essay turned out to be a bridge piece for me. I was trying out autobiographical writing; it felt awfully good. I was opening myself to different kinds of writing and exploring subjects about which I never used to allow myself even to think. I was experimenting in print with ethnic identity, talking for the first time in my writing about being an Italian American woman. I hadn't abandoned ties with my family or denied ethnicity in daily life: I looked Italian, cooked Italian, and observed many Italian customs. But now, for the first time, as I connected my work with my personal history, I saw being Italian American as part of my life as a teacher and writer.

I

The Godfather appeared in March 1969 and made publishing history. It rose quickly on the best-seller lists and stayed on those lists for an unprecedented sixty-nine weeks. *Newsweek* and *Time* were among the first magazines to publish reviews. The most prestigious and coveted of reviews, in the *New York Times Book Review,* appeared on April 27, but only after Puzo's novel had been on the paper's best-seller list for four weeks and had risen to the number-two spot.

The early reviews offered shamefully little insight into the novel, commenting rather simplistically on its portrayal of the Mafia. *Time,* for example, found the moral of the novel to be that "the Family that preys together, stays together": in other words, "crime pays." Dick Schaap's *New York Times* review suggested that what Philip "Roth has done for masturbation" in *Portnoy's Complaint* (number one the week of April 27), "Puzo has done for murder." Schaap's comparison is off-the-cuff and glib; but if we stick with it, we can recognize some interesting features of the literary scene in 1969.[1]

Like Roth's book, Puzo's reflected the power of ethnicity in American literature, with the groups represented more numerous by the late sixties than ever before.[2] Also like Roth's book, *The Godfather* occupied the middle ground between what the bookstores call "fiction" and what they call "literature." But coming from the Italian American community, Puzo's novel had less support in the publishing and academic establishments, less chance to move into the esteemed category of "literature" than did the novel by the better-known Roth. Reviews of Puzo's book—in contrast now to those for Roth—rarely made the front page or a primary position in magazines and newspapers. The *New York Times* notice appeared on page thirty-four, under the irrelevant caption "At Cosa Nostra, business was booming." Its lightheartedness insulted the novel, as when the reviewer advised the reader: "Pick a night with nothing good on television, and you'll come out far ahead."

There are several reasons why Roth was indeed "better known," reasons having little to do with abstract ideas of literary quality. Among these was his affiliation with a prestigious university. Even more significantly, publishers, reviewers, readers, and teachers knew how to classify him: he belongs to the Jewish American literary tradition rather than to the Italian American literary tradition. If you have asked yourself, "the Italian American literary tradition?" you are right to do so and have proved my point.

The Jewish and Italian immigrant experiences were remarkably similar in this country during the twentieth century. Both groups arrived in large numbers during the same decades, with the majority of immigrants from relatively impoverished regions (eastern Europe, southern Italy) rather than from regions perceived as "elite" (Germany, northern Italy). They settled by and large in the same northeastern cities, often sharing the same neighborhoods and the same kinds of employment (in, for example, the garment industry, in which both my Italian American mother and Jewish mother-in-law worked). The compatibility of the two cultures continues today, with intermarriages frequent. But their experiences in America very soon began to move at different paces.

Although equally poor, European Jews brought with them a tradition steeped in the value of education and learning. They entered American systems of higher education and produced, in a relatively short time, teachers, publishers, and writers. Most Italian immigrants, as Puzo notes, "were illiterate, as were their parents before them, their Italian not even that of their native literary tradition."[3] Sicilians were especially suspicious of all "systems" and reluctant to believe that their children could become the "padroni" of the New World. Like Puzo's mother, they felt on their pulses that "artistic beauty after all could spring only from the seedbed of fine clothes, fine food, luxurious living," and not from the northeast's immigrant communities (*Godfather Papers*, 13). An anecdote Puzo tells about his mother illustrates beautifully this side of the Italian American temperament: when Puzo called her to tell her that he was being offered huge sums for *The Godfather* after years of penury, his mother's only comment was, "Don't tell nobody" (*Godfather Papers*, 37).

In the first generations, Italian Americans chose a modest version of the American dream: they preferred a secure working-class living to reaching for wealth or upper-middle-class status. "Books" and "learning" treatened the solidarity of family necessary for survival in dangerous times. For among many Italian Americans, it was customary for children to leave school at the earliest opportunity, to take jobs in factories and offices, to supplement their parents' incomes. Even the free university system of New York could not tempt many Italian Americans to bypass the immediate financial well-being of their families for a future gain that was, after all, only potential. Italian Americans entered higher education and the literary professions later than Jews; indeed, a significant representation of Italian Americans in university teaching, publishing, and writing has emerged only recently. Roth has repeatedly, and brilliantly, made much of how what he wrote made him a maverick for many Jews. Puzo's decision to write, quite independent of what he wrote, made him a maverick in his generation, in his mother's vernacular, someone who "had gone off his nut" (*Godfather Papers*, 15).

In a world where "literary quality" indisputably announced itself, factors such as the respective temperaments and economic lives of Jewish and Italian immigrants would be irrelevant. We do not live in such a world. By 1969, without there being any sinister conspiracy, the Jewish American tradition in literature was well-established, prolific, and diverse—as well as published, reviewed, read, discussed, and taught. The presence of Jewish Americans in these worlds made it natural and inevitable that Jewish American literature would interest publishers, teachers, and readers. The Italian American tradition scarcely existed. The availability of novels about the two immigrant experiences can serve as a quick index. How many there are for Jewish American culture! For Italian American culture there is virtually only Puzo's *The Fortunate Pilgrim,* which sold a mere three thousand copies when first published, despite its brilliance.

Recent discussions of canon formation have made it clear that powerful groups tend to canonize one of their own—after all, he is most likely to write a work that speaks to them. In an important article, Richard Ohmann has shown, for example, that novels chronicling the midlife crises of business or professional men were the standard subject of writers from the sixties who were becoming canonical by the early 1980s, writers like John Cheever and John Updike.[4] More radically, he suggests that their novels appeal to publishers and academicians precisely because their protagonists' dilemmas match those of leaders in the publishing and academic establishment—who are also, by and large, white, middle-class, Protestant, professional, and male.

Within U.S. culture, it is easy to recognize the hegemonic power of WASPs. It is harder, and more delicate, to define the position of Jews in the literary establishment. A minority? Well, yes—and a vital, invigorating one. And no—a powerful force that has earned (and had to earn) the power it now enjoys. It is neither a sinister conspiracy nor pure accident that Cheever's *Bullet Park* made the first page of the *New York Times Book Review* in the same issue that Puzo was reviewed on page thirty-four as a kind of joke. It is neither conspiratorial nor accidental that Roth has made that front page several times while Puzo has not, even after the great success of *The Godfather.*

Ironically, Puzo himself has tended to validate the system by which *The Godfather* is considered "fiction" rather than "literature." In published comments, he has said that he wrote *The Godfather* for money and that he "wrote below [his] gifts in that novel" (*Godfather Papers,* 41). At first, I was inclined to believe him, not just about his having written the book for money (an unchallengeable statement), but about its relatively low literary quality as compared to his other novels. To be sure, there are some very good things in *Dark Arena,* and *The Fortunate Pilgrim* is (aside from a slack opening) virtually perfect. *The Sicilian* is also a fine novel, with sophisticated plays on other kinds of literature, such as epic. But putting praise for Puzo's other novels aside, there remains the question: what's wrong with *The Godfather?* Nothing, I think, but its astonishing popularity and financial success. Puzo was a writer accustomed to suffering in the Flaubertian-Joycean tradition. He was educated in the classics, and self-described as "a true believer in art." Puzo could not help but be a little suspicious of, even contemptuous of, his most popular novel. Art isn't supposed to pay, isn't supposed to make the writer's life easier. It follows, then, at some level for Puzo, that *The Godfather* cannot be art but must be the book he wrote to enable him to continue the pursuit of art. Yet *The Godfather* is a remarkable achievement. And it can lay claim to being the world's most typical novel,[5] in part because of its vast popularity.

As the novel has become respectable as art, best-sellers have become suspect. What appeals to the masses is often assumed to be beneath the status of high literature, to be, by definition, outside the canon. Even Roth has suffered from this situation, with works like *The Ghost Writer* full of anxiety about their relationship to "the great tradition." Studies of Roth's works are available, but often written at banal thematic levels (the Jewish mother in Roth, the Jewish father in Roth, and so on)—the junk heap of literary criticism.[6] But Puzo, in part because he is an Italian American, has suffered more, receiving virtually no critical attention as a serious author. The situation is ironic, since the novel, perhaps more than any other kind of literature, has always blurred the distinction between popular and high art.

Because it was born after the invention of the printing press, the novel has always existed under the conditions of mass production.[7] It has depended on cheap mass production and circulating libraries. The novel has never been associated with patronage systems of production, but with the conditions of the marketplace, what the English call "Grub Street."

Major novelists of the nineteenth century often enjoyed vast popularity—Dickens being the most obvious example. Popularity was a condition of fulfilling the novel's two main ideals up to the mid-nineteenth century—entertainment and moral instruction. Only in the twentieth century did popularity come to imply lack of artistic quality, as writers like James, Joyce, and Woolf made popularity suspect. It is true that their novels downplay fictional elements with popular appeal—a fast-paced plot, for example, and accessible characters. But even these authors yearned for large sales and regretted the sacrifice of readership for artfulness: James, for example, always wanted to write a theatrical hit; Woolf counted and recounted sales anxiously.[8] In thriving artistically while selling well, Dickens and Puzo are, overall, more typical novelists than the modernist trio.

Still affordably priced (price is far from negligible in these matters), *The Godfather* continues to be widely read, its sales fueled by the popularity of the filmed version, a popular rental in today's ubiquitous video stores. The paperback's cover wisely proclaims the novel's fabled status as a best-seller, indicating to us its typicality as a novel, a claim that can be justified as well on a number of other, more intellectual, grounds.

II

In his classic essay "Manners, Morals, and the Novel," Lionel Trilling said that novels give the "feel" of a culture. Novels, said Trilling, convey a culture's hum and buzz of implication . . . the whole evanescent context in which its explicit statements are made . . . [the] half-uttered or unuttered or unutterable expressions of value . . . the things that for good or bad draw the people of a culture together and that separate them from the people of another culture.[9]

In the same way, the Russian critic Mikhail Bakhtin describes how a novel "must be a comprehensive reflection of its era," representing "all the social and ideological voices of its era, that is, all the era's languages that have any claim to being significant."[10]

The Godfather gives us the hum and buzz of Italian American culture, quite apart from its portrayal of the distinct and much smaller subculture of the Mafia. Specifically, it portrays Italian American culture in the decade from 1945 to 1955. This decade initiated massive changes in Italian American life, among them the increased presence of Italian Americans in writing, publishing, and universities. Like historical novels, *The Godfather* shows how "the past is the concrete precondition of the present."[11] It shows how Italian Americans got from their relative cultural isolation in 1945 into the mainstream.

In 1945, as the novel opens, Michael Corleone is a returned war veteran, attending Dartmouth College, then as now a bastion of WASP culture. Attendance at college presumes his separation from the family business—even if that business were to be the production of olive oil rather than crime. It has further encouraged a love affair with a Protestant daughter of New England, since college-educated Italian American girls, like the novel's Lucy Mancini, are rare.[12] The Italian American community is aware of these changes: Michael's entrance to Dartmouth (as opposed to the more expected, because local, City University, New York University, or Columbia) translates, in the community's terms, into having "left his father's house." Kay Adams appears to the group a "washed-out rag of an American girl," her manner "too free for a maiden" (18). Lucy's morals are suspect as "thoroughly Americanized." In Bakhtinian terms, the values and the language of the traditional Italian American infiltrate the novel. To people outside the Italian American community, the distinction between Italian and American would seem spurious, especially since Lucy is, like most younger guests at the wedding, American-born. To outsiders, attending college would seem natural, even desirable, with a college education implying nothing about a young woman's "reputation."

The boom in higher education in the decade following Sputnik would open the world of scholarships and degrees to Italian American children. I was part of that generation; Lucy Mancini and Michael Corleone represent the wave of the future. In the novel, the brave new world of education is welcomed, even courted. Michael Corleone, like his father Vito, desires the Americanization of his children because it will dictate their exit from the subculture of the Mafia. As the first Godfather tells his cohorts, "Some of you have sons who are professors, scientists, musicians, and you are fortunate" (293). What the novel does not say, but what lurks within its pages, is that the process of Americanization, carried to its logical conclusion, would represent the end of Italian American culture as it had existed in the prewar decades. It would mean intermarriages like Michael's with Kay, or, even more typically, like Lucy's with Jules Segal. It would mean moving away from the old neighborhoods, establishing cross-country networks of family that minimize closeness and reduce the frequency of family gatherings for dinner that is a hallmark of Italian American culture. *The Godfather* chronicles a moment when Italian Americans—as something quite separate, I must stress, from the Mafia—were assimilating with the majority culture.

The Chinese have a curse that runs something like "May

you get what you wish." For Vito Corleone, the curse if fulfilled would have meant the passing of his empire from the family as his sons entered the mainstream of American life, becoming part of the world the novel calls the "pezzonovanti," and the sixties called "the military-industrial complex." The dialect and customs of the Sicilians would be displaced by the Florentine Italian taught in universities and by the homogenizing forces of American suburbia, so similar whether in New York, California, Illinois, or North Carolina. Less progressive than Vito Corleone, Puzo's mother was baffled by her son's literary ambitions, and she urged him to work instead for the railroads in Hell's Kitchen, an immigrant neighborhood.[13] My own mother could not understand my desire to go to college, thinking that I should instead become a secretary. She trusted that job's financial security and tendency to be relinquished upon motherhood. She rightly sensed (I see now in retrospect) that college would remove me from her world. *The Godfather* thus captures a key point of transition for Italian Americans and the ambivalence often surrounding the idea of college until well into the 1960s.

VITO CORLEONE SPEAKS OF SONS who are musicians, scientists, professors—not of daughters. In the same way, as late as 1993, Gay Talese discussed the situation of Italian American writers without mentioning a female other than Camille Paglia—and even her very briefly.[14] Like Talese's article, Vito Corleone's speech reflects a significant part of Italian American culture—its emphasis on males and denigration of females. The novel's opening masterfully and subtly establishes the relative spheres of men and women.

The Godfather begins not with the direct presentation of the title character but with a series of indirect approaches to him. In this it rivals other narrative examples, such as the *Odyssey* and *Madame Bovary,* whose openings also delay the presentation of the main character. The novel begins with three vignettes about Italian American men with problems—the undertaker Amerigo Bonasera, the singer Johnny Fontane, and the baker Nazorine. Although the three come from different social strata, each has a problem with the customs, laws, or bureaucracies of the majority culture, and each reaches an identical conclusion: that the Old World mechanisms of the Godfather can help when the institutions of the New World have failed. This is, indeed, the primary point of the opening vignettes.

But they have another point as well. When one looks to the root of each man's problem, one finds a woman—Bonasera's daughter who has taken up with American boys; Fontane's second wife, an actress, a non-Italian, and a "tramp"; Nazorine's "hot number" of a daughter, who requires prompt marrying to the Italian prisoner of war assigned to her father's shop. Each man's trouble comes from his association with women. The novel continues this pattern, most crucially in Sonny's vulnerability on the night he is killed racing to rescue his sister.

Responding to Fontane, the Godfather expressly makes the point that men ought not to take women too seriously. What is Johnny to do? In his most passionate declaration in the novel, the Godfather tells Johnny that he must "start by acting like a man . . . `LIKE A MAN!'" He warns Johnny not to "let women dictate your actions . . . [because] they are not competent in this world, though certainly they will be saints in heaven while we men burn in hell" (36–37). Most of all, he urges Johnny to cultivate the value of male friendships, urging upon him his power to help his boyhood friend, Nino.

The novel reinforces the Don's sense of woman's place in multiple ways. The action proper begins with a wedding, as Connie does what good Italian girls are supposed to do: marries a fellow Italian (albeit a worthless non-Sicilian), transferring her father's power over her to her husband, a power with which even Don Corleone will not interfere. For that wedding, the Corleone women cook, though their immense wealth might free them from such menial duties. Above all, women are not to know, and not to ask, about "business." That is the key lesson that Kay must learn as a wife. The need for women's ignorance is more pressing in the world of crime than in others, but the Mafia world is a microcosm of Italian American society in this regard. Men and male lines of affiliation count; women play a secondary and supportive role, a role more or less separate from their men's.

In its traditional attitudes towards women, Italian American culture magnified the more general views of postwar American culture. While writing this essay, I chanced to see the old movie *Father of the Bride* and was reminded of how pervasively and consistently the fifties iterated and reiterated lessons about men's and women's proper roles. But the strong patriarchal models embedded in traditional Italian life served more than a representational role in *The Godfather,* which was published in 1969—not in the forties or fifties. Nineteen sixty-nine was a year of bra-burnings and demonstrations, of the movement then called "women's liberation," when one hot issue was whether to use "Ms." or "Miss" and "Mrs." The movement was a frequent topic of conversation, soon to be a common subject on popular television situation comedies like *All in the Family, The Mary Tyler Moore Show,* and *Maude.* Nineteen sixty-nine was a year when it was possible to be called, with no irony intended, "A women's lib dame." While it is difficult to say for sure, one suspects that the novel's treatment of women had a special appeal in 1969 for an audience uneasy about women's new assertiveness. By portraying the macho world of the Mafia, the novel served as both fantasy and wish fulfillment, and as a way of coping with changing patterns of gender relationships.

The emphasis on male power so pervasive in *The Godfather* has had distinct and in many ways undesirable consequences for Italian American culture, as well as consequences in my own life that make me especially sensitive to it. When, in 1983, the *New York Times Magazine* featured a cover story on Italian Americans' entry into powerful positions, it was striking to me that most of the portraits were of men.[15] Almost all the Italian American women of achievement were traditional enough to be married and to have taken their husbands' names. But they were not, by and large, married to Italian Americans. As a female born in Brooklyn in 1949, my own attitudes towards being Italian American are considerably more ambivalent than those of males I know. In fact, the first time I used my family name (as middle name) in a published piece was when I originally published this essay; before that, I associated my Italian heritage with hostility to my desire to read, teach, and write. It is difficult to prove, except by anecdotal evidence, how strongly Italian American culture in the period and place covered by Puzo's novel resisted the idea of college and careers for women, even while beginning to entertain those ideas for men. But Puzo's novel provides traces of such evidence, and even anecdotes can be compelling. So let me give one, by quoting a young man, an Italian American soon to be college-bound, who informed me, in the sixties (echoing the movie *Marty* in all seriousness), that "college girls are one step above the gutter."

Ironically, the first Italian American to achieve nomination to national office as vice president was a woman, Geraldine Ferraro. Was it an accident that her campaign began to falter when she attempted a joke, with reference to her husband's reluctance to make his tax returns public, about what Italian men are "like"? Ferraro stresses the importance of her remark, saying that "my candidacy had been struck an almost fatal blow. . . . And I had done it to myself."[16] She blames herself, but she did not really "do it to herself." She spoke from the "hum and buzz" of her culture, a culture that, however well it served her in other ways, led her in this key regard into a major gaffe. The issues raised by Ferraro's case seem to me relevant and, indeed, embodied in Puzo's portrayal of Italian American culture.

Other hums and buzzes of Italian American life inform the novel. Sick friends and relatives, especially friends of one's parents, must be visited in the hospital. Frequent phone calls to the family are a requirement, their cessation an insult. Honor, especially male honor as vested in females, has paramount value; "respect" is a primary good, which must be shown in a variety of appropriate ways. The novel shows these aspects of Italian American culture at large as clearly as it reveals, more obviously and sensationally, the hum and buzz of Mafia life: the organization of regimes, the conduct of wars, the rules governing civilians, the meaning of a dead fish sent as a message. The Mafia rules have gotten the most attention from reviewers and the general public, and for good reason. Learning how to survive in an exotic world has been an established lure of the novel from *Robinson Crusoe* through the novels of Louis L'Amour. But one learns, from this novel, much that is as natural as breathing to Italian Americans. Along with Kay Adams, non-Italian readers learn what Italian Americans know by acculturation, such as "how important it was to do such things [as visit the hospital] if you wanted to get along with the old Italians" (113).[17]

One of the subtler features of Italian American culture powerful in the novel is what I call the power of euphemism. Italian American culture is much concerned with respect, honor, and decorum, believing that some things should be thought but not said outside the family. In this, Italian American culture resembles Southern culture in America, whose love of cliché and euphemism and of leaving things unspoken is a major theme of writers like Faulkner and O'Connor. When assessing privately his daughter's situation, for example, Nazorine the baker thinks "lewdly": "He had seen her brush her swelling buttocks against Enzo's front when the baker's helper squeezed behind her to fill the counter baskets with hot loaves from the oven. The young rascal's hot loaf would be in *her* oven if proper steps were not taken" (15). What he says to the Godfather is quite different in tone, though its meaning is fully understood: "The baker told the story of his daughter and Enzo. A fine Italian lad from Sicily; captured by the American Army; sent to the United States as a prisoner of war; given parole to help our war effort! A pure and honorable love had sprung up between honest Enzo and his sheltered Katherine but now that the war was ended the poor lad would be repatriated to Italy and Nazorine's daughter would surely die of a broken heart" (22–23). Etiquette requires that the Godfather listen without comment to the whole story and not question the romantic narrative chosen by Nazorine, with its poor lads and maidens pure in mind and body. A master of euphemism himself, the Don would not be tempted.

At the peace meeting of the five families and the national chiefs (a miniature in mock-epic style), the Don himself spectacularly uses euphemism and equivocation. In the first example, he assures Michael's safe return to America:

"I am a superstitious man, a ridiculous failing but I must confess it here. And so if some unlucky accident should befall my youngest son, if some police officer should accidentally shoot him, if he should hang himself in his cell . . . my superstition will make me feel that it was the result of the ill will still borne me by some people here. Let me go further. If my son is struck by a bolt of lightning I will blame some of the people here. If his plane should fall into the sea or his ship sink beneath the waves of the ocean, if he should catch a mortal fever, if his automobile should be struck by a train, such is my superstition that I would blame the ill will felt by people here." (293–94)

In the second example, he sets in motion a plan for revenge and for reestablishing his family's preeminence:

> "What manner of men are we then, if we do not have our reason? . . . We are all no better than beasts in a jungle if that were the case. But we have reason, we can reason with each other and we can reason with ourselves. To what purpose should we start all these troubles again, the violence and the turmoil? My son is dead and that is a misfortune and I must bear it, not make the innocent world around me suffer with me. And so I say, I give my honor, that I will never seek vengeance, I will never seek knowledge of the deeds that have been done in the past." (292)

Don Corleone signals his willingness to live by the code of euphemism: his oldest son is dead, not murdered by some of those present at the meeting. But anyone who misses the equivocation in the Don's long speech will have trouble understanding the rest of the novel and be in a mess of trouble in a Mafia war—for the Don's emphatic stress on his not seeking revenge in no way binds Michael or precludes his helping Michael to plan revenge. As long as Vito Corleone no longer leads his family, revenge can be taken with impunity, despite his oath. The power of decorous speech and euphemism can be harmless or deadly, mild or powerful. But it is an important part of the culture of this novel.

Ultimately, however, *The Godfather* says something not just about the small, specialized Mafia world or the larger, non-Mafia world of first- and second-generation Italian Americans, but about the still larger worlds in which these exist. And here euphemism functions as social commentary. The Don sees and refers to his organization as a "business." Indeed, he urges the Mafia chiefs "to be cunning like the business people, there's more money in it and it's better for our children and grandchildren" (293). The Don doesn't make threats, he talks "reason" to his opponents or (in the code phrase America adopted from Francis Ford Coppola's film), he "makes offers you can't refuse."

The narrative voice frequently adopts this language of euphemism:

> Like many businessmen of genius he [Don Corleone] learned that free competition was wasteful, monopoly efficient. And so he simply set about achieving that efficient monopoly.
>
> • • • •
>
> When an employee of his was arrested and sent to prison by some mischance, that unfortunate man's family received a living allowance. (213, 215)

The Don Corleone of the Depression years emerges, through the language of euphemism, as an Italian American, slightly unorthodox Franklin Delano Roosevelt, a sainted figure in the working-class areas of New York:

> Everywhere in the city, honest men begged for honest work in vain. Proud men demeaned themselves and their families to accept official charity from a contemptuous officialdom. But the men of Don Corleone walked the streets with their heads held high . . . with no fear of losing their jobs. (215)

Late in the novel, in a crucial passage, Michael tells Kay what she absolutely must know to understand his father:

> My father is a businessman trying to provide for his wife and children and those friends he might need someday in a time of trouble. He doesn't accept the rules of the society we live in because those rules would have condemned him to a life not suitable to a man like himself, a man of extraordinary force and character. What you have to understand is that he

considers himself the equal of all those great men like Presidents and Prime Ministers and Supreme Court Justices and Governors of the States. (365)

In this regard, the novel's postwar setting is important. As the Don pointedly asks, "After all, are we or are we not better men than those *pezzonovanti* who have killed countless millions of men in our lifetimes?" (294).

To see these statements, as some early reviewers saw them, as justifying or prettifying the Mafia is to miss the point. Michael senses that the Mafia in this country will go the corrupt way of the Sicilian Mafia: it will be not an organization of Robin Hoods supporting good King Richard (the Lion-Hearted, Cor-leone), but an organization serving the King Johns of the world, "a degenerate capitalist structure" (328). Far from justifying the Mafia, the novel's comparisons of Mafia business to ordinary business condemn the latter.

If the bottom line counts most and the "me" generation knows it, if employees can be exploited, if executives can be fired late in life, if profit controls all, if men are asked to sacrifice family life for business success and corporations take no responsibility for child care or wives' careers, then "legitimate" business functions by some of the same ethical codes as the most degraded forms of the Mafia. The hum and buzz of the novel's mafiosi are not as different as we might think from the hum and buzz of Wall Street and the bastions of capitalism—though Wall Street stops short of murder by hire. That is the more radical, more interesting implication to be drawn from this aspect of the novel.

III

A typical theme of novels, subject to infinite variation, is the theme of the Bildungsroman: the growth or development of a character (usually a young adult) as he/she moves from innocence to experience and comes to share the knowledge always available to the author of the novel.[18] Usually, the character either dies or learns how to survive in society, how to make the adjustments and compromises a social existence demands. Since the society in which novels take place is almost always bourgeois and capitalist, the protagonist is, in essence, taught how to live as a good bourgeois. Insofar as novels teach readers these kinds of lessons, novels have been powerful instruments of socialization.

The Godfather includes two such patterns: the first, and more important, involves Michael Corleone, the second Kay Adams. In this bifurcation of the innocence-to-experience theme, and in assigning it to college-age characters of both genders, Puzo, perhaps without knowing it, has made the book a natural for college courses. He has also followed novelistic tradition, since the period of a protagonist's young adulthood forms the typical time span of novels.

A character's movement from innocence to experience can take two forms: the character can authentically change and be at the novel's end different from the way he/she was at the beginning, or the character can uncover his/her authentic self, piercing the veils of self-delusion. Michael's growth follows the second pattern, a pattern shared with such typical characters as Elizabeth Bennet in *Pride and Prejudice* and Pip in *Great Expectations*. We know, from the beginning of the novel, that Michael is a favorite son and sense that he is like his father, even before Michael himself perceives the implications of the similarity. The assault on Don Corleone brings out Michael's true colors. For example, when he is asked to man the phones rather than to become involved in the conflict, Michael "felt awkward, almost ashamed, and he noticed Clemenza and Tessio with faces so carefully impassive that he was sure that they were hiding their contempt" (99).

Significantly, Michael's entrance into the family requires adopting the clan's distance from women, moving away from honesty with Kay, and dissipating erotic energy. When Michael calls Kay after his father's wounding to say he will be late, Kay banters in their usual fashion, but Michael cannot reciprocate:

> "All right," Kay said. "I'll be waiting. Can I do any Christmas shopping for you? Or anything else?"
> "No," Michael said. "Just be ready."
> She gave a little excited laugh. "I'll be ready," she said. "Aren't I always?"
> "Yes, you are," he said. "That's why you're my best girl."
> "I love you," she said. "Can you say it?"
> Michael looked at the four hoods sitting in the kitchen. "No," he said. "Tonight, OK?" (114)

Even before Michael meets McCluskey, the bad cop, at the hospital—the man he eventually murders—Michael puts "the family" above Kay. He shows favorable signs for his vocation.

After Michael kills McCluskey, he is sent to Sicily to avoid arrest. There, in book 6, he discovers his destiny, in a sequence that parallels Vito Corleone's history in book 3. Sicily not only makes Michael "understand his father's character," it also (when Michael's bride, Appolonia, is murdered) gives him an immediate and tangible need for revenge. Michael signals the fullness of his development by sending the message that he wants to be his father's son. The message says it all. After it, Michael will lie repeatedly to Kay and he will fully enter the Mafia world with the intention of controlling it. His destiny, his uncovering of his true self, is complete.

Once we recognize the importance of the Bildungsroman pattern for Michael Corleone, we can see that the novel's title is fundamentally ambiguous. At the beginning it refers to Vito Corleone, at the end to Michael. In serving as godfather to

Carlo Rizzi's son, and then ordering Carlo's death, Michael emblematizes the double face of godfatherhood: protective and nurturing, deadly and cruel. The broken nose he sustains from McCluskey is the visible sign of his duplicity, a sign with which Michael is reluctant to part, a sign of his entry into family life and of the still unavenged attacks on his father and brother Sonny.

By necessity in this male-centered novel, Kay's development is secondary in importance. Yet she more authentically undergoes a change in personality, moving from a playful, open, liberated college girl into the role of Mafia wife. Oddly, and perhaps a bit subversively, Puzo suggests that the WASP spirit that founded this nation resembles the Sicilian codes adhered to by the major characters. When Kay and her father face down the investigating policemen, refusing to reveal anything of Michael or to be blackmailed, they practice the equivalent of Sicilian *omertá*. Most of what she needs to learn is, however, unnatural to Kay. And so she gets a tutor in the novel, in the unlikely figure of Mama Corleone.

Mrs. Corleone at first assumes that Kay, quite simply, is not good material for a Mafia wife. When Kay comes to ask about Michael after the McCluskey murder, the mother kisses the girl and advises her to "forget about Mikey, he no the man for you." Kay realizes that euphemism has been eloquent, "that the young man she had loved was a cold-blooded murderer. And that she had been told by the most unimpeachable source: his mother" (238). But Michael's mother changes her mind about Kay and is instrumental in bringing them together. She changes her mind because Kay calls repeatedly to ask about Michael, and because she sees changes she does not like in Michael after his return from Sicily. The mother-in-law then becomes the daughter-in-law's guide to Italian American life, teaching her how to fry peppers, how to mesh into the network of visitations to and from relatives' houses on the mall, how to attend church and to pray for her husband's soul.

When Michael orders the execution of his brother-in-law, Carlo Rizzi, in the orgy of death near the end of the novel, Kay has to accept the unimportance of female values in the Mafia world. For like Connie, Carlo's wife, Kay believes that Carlo should be forgiven even though he has caused Sonny Corleone's death. When Kay decides, at the end of the novel, to return to Michael, she accepts her new role in life, her own destiny as someone unable to judge or control the direction of her world. In *Godfather II*, the film script has her change her mind. But I cannot help but feel that that change belies the truth of the original novel. Kay's decision, once made, will be final.

The Godfather's adherence to the Bildungsroman theme is thus strong, though it is not complete. The difference comes in the extent to which, unlike the Bildungsroman in general, *The Godfather* teaches the protagonists to conform to the rules of a specialized society (the Mafia) rather than to the norms of bourgeois life. Recognizing the deviation helps point to a final way that *The Godfather* is a typical novel: its ability to harken back to earlier forms of storytelling and to incorporate them into the new form.

IV

Novels are often compared to the kinds of storytelling that preceded them historically: epic and romance. European critics, preeminently Lukács, but also Bakhtin, Stanzel, and Goldmann, see the novel as replacing the epic, which was linked to a belief in gods and to a view of heroism no longer possible in modern culture.[19] Anglo-American critics have tended, by contrast, to see the novel as "anti-romance," as opposed to the romance's elevation of love, heroism, and adventure and its will to a happy ending.[20] Such definitions of the novel are in many ways quite helpful. But it is perhaps best to recognize the novel as a polyphonic genre containing chords from both epic and romance. In fact, *The Godfather* is in some ways a version of Homer's *Odyssey* for our time—the *Odyssey* being "the epic of love," or a hybrid of epic and romance.

The *Odyssey* begins, not with the introduction of Odysseus, but with the dilemma of his son, Telemachus. Telemachus is eighteen and his manhood has produced a crisis in Ithaca. For he is now eligible to assume his father's throne, left vacant for the long years of Odysseus's absence, and coveted as well by Penelope's many suitors. Having already arranged for Odysseus's return, Athene appears to Telemachus in order to offer him some key advice. She tells him: "It is a wise son who knows his own father." That formulation signals the identity theme that operates in subtle ways throughout the subsequent narrative.[21]

Athene advises Telemachus to journey to his father's old comrades, who tell him stories of his father's past that help him mature. Notice already how the father-son theme of *The Godfather* repeats the pattern of the *Odyssey*, with substantial niceties such as Michael's journey to his father's Sicily (parallel to Telemachus's journey) and Michael's crucial utterance that he "wishes to be his father's son" (parallel to Athene's advice). Knowing who you are, in both works, means understanding one's father and sharing his ideas and strength. Each son, Telemachus and Michael, needs to demonstrate his similarity to his father in a major test: Telemachus when he shows the ability to string his father's bow and fights by his side; Michael when he is ready to step into the Godfather's role and orchestrate his father's complex plan for revenge.

The middle portion of the *Odyssey*, the most famous portion, portrays Odysseus's adventures in his ten years of traveling—ten years also being the time span of *The Godfather* (Puzo, we might remember, studied Classics). In the *Odyssey*, Odysseus narrates these past events to his hosts on Phaecaia. Although book 3 of *The Godfather* does not have the same narrative form, or length, or weight, it shares the quality of retrospective narration and interrupts with the father's history the forward motion of the present-day plot.

When Odysseus finally returns to Ithaca, he reveals himself to his son, collaborating with Telemachus about how to avenge himself on Penelope's suitors. This collaboration resembles Don Corleone's collaboration with Michael after he returns from Sicily. Both plans involve seeming mildly submissive and disguising intentions until the moment for revenge is ripe. No one—especially Penelope/especially Kay—must know all the details of the plan except for the father and son. In both works, key parts of the plan are confided to trusted male associates who have proved their loyalty by a lifetime of service. In each work, the success of the plan constitutes the dramatic climax. A massive slaughter occurs, in which the father/son team achieves victory by superior cunning and strength. No mercy is shown to enemies. In Homer, however, female allies of the enemies are also killed, while in Puzo, "civilian" females are untouchable, part of the Mafia code.

The epic "war" themes accomplished, both works turn to the romance theme of married love—Odysseus is as yet unreconciled to Penelope, Michael's revenge has ruptured his relationship to Kay. In a long and weighty scene, Odysseus negotiates with Penelope, assuring her that he is the husband she has waited for and that he is willing to respect her will and her power.[22] She accepts him, the token of acceptance being the symbolic marriage bed, whose posts sink into the Ithacan earth. The epic ends when Odysseus and Telemachus, who have massed with their followers to meet the families of the slain suitors and anticipate a new slaughter, find out that they don't have to fight. In fact, the gods prohibit further revenge and dispense blessed forgetfulness of past wrongs.

Here *The Godfather* both follows and does not follow the earlier epic. Kay does accept Michael in his new, godlike, role as Godfather, but she negotiates with the lawyer, Tom Hagen, not with Michael; the joyous affirmation of marriage in the earlier work is dissipated and shadowed, Kay's role more passive than Penelope's. There are no intervening gods in *The Godfather* to end the cycle of revenge and to dispense forgetfulness of blood feuds. Michael's power will face other challenges, necessitate other massacres. The future is likely to hold repetition of the past, despite Michael's plan to make the family businesses legitimate. Indeed, the cycle of violence repeats in the film sequels to *The Godfather*—and this is entirely consistent with the spirit of the novel.

Like many Greek works (the *Oresteia* and the *Iliad* among them), and like many epics (such as *Beowulf*), the *Odyssey* describes transitions from ties of blood, family, and vendetta to the rules of law, communal good, and government. Novels do not usually address the issue of blood versus law—for that issue has usually been decided before the eighteenth century, when novels became a recognizable form. But novels are not precluded from recording the conflict between layers of culture—indeed, the historical novels of Scott are celebrated for doing so.[23] And quite typically, novels teach the hero of a Bildungsroman to reject earlier modes of heroism and settle for being an ordinary man.[24]

At the beginning of *The Godfather* and again at the end, Michael Corleone aspires to be a good citizen and businessman—like the typical hero of novels. In a sense, he is again following Vito Corleone's example, since the original Godfather had begun to move the family assets into politics and law. Ironically, if Michael had become that good citizen and businessman, and if Puzo had waited until Michael had reached middle age to write about him, the novel might have had a better chance of being not just a best-seller, but a novel recognized as "literature" and, ultimately, a canonical text. For then, like Updike and Cheever, Puzo would have been writing a novel that spoke to the experiences of the men in the board room and commuter trains. Instead, Michael gets a role that fits the model of good citizen and businessman only within the microcosmic world of the Mafia and which is tinged (in its power over blood, not just money) by earlier, epic patterns of blood heroism. And Puzo gets a book that sells well but has not, as yet, become canonical. People who take novels seriously—and not just Italian Americans—ought to give it a second look. For in its reach, in its exploration of the Bildungsroman theme, in its revelation of competing language and cultural systems, and in crossing between popular and high art, *The Godfather* can clearly be shown to be one of the world's most typical novels.

Notes

1. Dick Schapp, "Review of *The Godfather*," *New York Times Book Review*, April 27, 1969, 34–35. See unsigned review of *The Godfather*, *Time* Magazine, March 14, 1969, 103–4.

2. The new ethnic strength of American literature raises, perhaps inevitably, the responsibility of the writer towards his ethnic group: will it, for example, hurt the group if writers use stereotypes that express national prejudice against the group? Would it be understood that such stereotypes do not represent the group as a whole? Alternately, should the ethnic writer present only shining examples of his group? The commentary on Roth has been especially concerned with this issue, which Roth made a major theme of his Zuckerman trilogy. *The Godfather* raises similar issues about the confusion, in some minds, between Italian Americans in general and the very small membership of the Mafia. Early reviews speculated in a bizarre and inappropriate way, for example, on Puzo's knowledge of the Mafia.

3. Mario Puzo, *The Godfather Papers and Other Confessions* (New York: Fawcett, 1972), 13.

4. Richard Ohmann, "The Shaping of a Canon: U.S. Fiction, 1960–1975," *Critical Inquiry* (September 1983): 199–223.

5. In a landmark essay, Victor Shklovsky made a similar claim for *Tristram Shandy*, noting that "the assertion that *Tristram Shandy* is not a novel is common: for persons who make that statement, opera alone is music—a symphony is chaos. *Tristram Shandy* is the most typical novel in world literature." See "Sterne's *Tristram Shandy*: Stylistic Commentary," in *Readings in Russian Poetics*, eds. Ladislav Matejka and Krystna Pomorska (Cambridge, Mass.: MIT Press, 1971), 57.

6. Published books on Roth are rudimentary; still, books about an author serve as one measure of academic respectability.

7. See M. M. Bakhtin, *The Dialogic Imagination: Four Essays by M. M. Bakhtin*, ed. Michael Holquist, trans. Caryl Emerson and Michael Holquist (Austin: University of Texas Press, 1981), 4–5, on this aspect of the novel's origins.

8. Woolf's diaries and letters are full of data about sales and sales receipts and of anxiety about whether her novels will be read.

9. Lionel Trilling, "Manners, Morals, and the Novel," in *The Liberal Imagination: Essays on Literature and Society* (New York: Viking, 1950), 206–7.

10. Bakhtin, *Dialogic Imagination*, 411.

11. The phrase is Georg Lukács's in *The Historical Novel*, trans. from the German by Hannah and Stanley Mitchell (New York: Humanities Press, 1965).

12. Puzo, *The Godfather* (New York: Putnam's, 1969), 21.

13. See Puzo, *Godfather Papers*, 24–25, for a revealing portrait of Puzo's family.

14. Gay Talese, "Where Are the Italian-American Novelists?", *New York Times Book Review*, March 1993. His piece excited a flurry of people critical of the omission of women. Still, there is a pragmatic explanation for Talese's omission: many Italian American women have married non-Italian men and taken their last names.

Among the writers Talese might have mentioned are Sandra M. Gilbert, Mary Gordon, Louise De Salvo, Barbara Grizzuti Harrison, and Helen Barolini.

15. G. G. Hall's essay, "Italian Americans: Coming into Their Own," *New York Times Magazine*, May 15, 1983, foretold America's recent fascination with figures like Iacocca, Scalia, and Cuomo.

16. Geraldine Ferraro (with Linda Bird Francke), *Ferraro: My Story* (New York: Bantam, 1985), 156.

17. Another character who functions in this way is Tom Hagen, who knows all the Mafia rules (he is, after all, consigliore), but still notices them because he is Irish and not Italian.

18. See, for two of many possible examples of literary criticism on this theme, Maurice Shroder, "The Novel as a Genre," in *The Theory of the Novel,* ed. Philip Stevick (New York: Free Press, 1967), 13–29, and Réné Girard, *Desire, Deceit, and the Novel,* trans. Yvonne Freccero (Baltimore: Johns Hopkins University Press, 1965).

19. The preeminent expression of this view is Georg Lukács's in *The Theory of the Novel: A Historico-Philosophical Essay on the Forms of Great Epic Literature,* trans. Anna Bostock (Cambridge, Mass.: MIT Press, 1971).

20. This tendency begins with the novel in England, and it is reflected in early definitions of the genre by Clara Reeve, Congreve, and Samuel Johnson. It continued to inform criticism of the novel through the nineteenth century and into the twentieth. Shroder's essay is a contemporary example. Northrop Frye's criticism also takes this contrast between novel and romance for granted.

21. On the identity theme, see G. E. Dimock, "The Name of Odysseus," in *Homer: A Collection of Critical Essays,* eds. George Steiner and Robert Fagles (Englewood Cliffs, N.J.: Prentice Hall, 1962), 106–21.

22. For a marvelous analysis of this scene and of gender reversals that prepare for it, see Helene P. Foley, "Reverse Similes and Sex Roles in *The Odyssey,*" *Arethusa II,* no. 1/2 (1978): 7–26.

23. See Lukács's landmark work on Scott in *The Historical Novel,* with its attention to how the modern British bourgeois state required the dismemberment of traditional Scottish clans.

24. This kind of play with epic, romance, and novelistic heroes characterizes, for example, Cervantes's *Don Quixote* (often considered the world's first novel) and Stendhal's *The Charterhouse of Parma,* a model of the interplay between realistic and romance-like narratives. Such persistent attention to past heroic models suggests that they have not lost their hold on the imagination of novelists and novel readers.

E i g h t

The Politics of the "We"

I

There is a kind of "we" that seems utterly convincing—rounded, magisterial, confident—and enough to make you want to die if you can't be part of it. This "we" is more than a pronoun. In fact, the pronoun is only the most obvious marker, the sign and symbol of how the circle of culture gets drawn: who's in, who's out; why; and to what effect.

Here, for example, is critic Georg Lukács, using an impressive "we" in his 1922 essay on reification, the process by which people become alienated from their work, cut off from psychic development, and turned into objects:

> There is . . . no way man can bring his physical and psychic "qualities" into play without their being subjected increasingly to this reifying process. We need only think of marriage, and without troubling to point to the developments of the nineteenth century we can remind ourselves of the way in which Kant, for example, described the situation.[1]

I admire Lukács's essay for its insights;[2] I envy its intellectual power. Yet I am also aware of discomfort when reading passages like this one. The "we" in this passage intimidates readers by testing knowledge and background, some of it fairly detailed: does Lukács accurately represent what Kant says about marriage, for example? What other nineteenth-century developments does Lukács have in mind? If these questions make you even the tiniest bit uncomfortable, that is one reason the critical "we" and its equivalents are so effective: they make readers *want* to pass the test—to be part of the community addressed, part of the in-group the writing defines. Intellectuals are especially vulnerable to the pressure this kind of "we" exerts: when references are unfamiliar, they have learned to smile, noncommittally.

"We" has traditionally been the pronoun of choice for popes, kings, and queens; for them, it comes with the territory of office. For critics, the trick in using it as a source of authority seems to be believing that the litany of great names comprises an aristocracy of its own, a line of descent as yet incomplete, awaiting one more name: "one of us" is missing in the "we," and the missing one is the writer himself. Whether or not the writer agrees fully with the powerful ancestors matters less than the fact of essential conversational relationship. The writer needs to feel a part of the we as naturally, as inevitably, as royal heirs entitled to the throne: born to it, no special effort involved.

But that serenely entitled "we" can be deceptively at odds with the facts. Consider once again my opening example, Georg Lukács. Lukács was a twentieth-century Hungarian Jew, the son of a wealthy banker, in Christian Eastern Europe.[3] The original family name was Lowinger, which was transposed into the Magyar tongue by Lukács's father, an assimilated Jew who sent his children to schools for upper-middle-class gentiles. Throughout his youth, Lukács felt alienated and alone—feelings that led to his first major work,

The Theory of the Novel, where he defines modernity as "transcendental homelessness"—a permanent condition of exile
and unease.[4] In his early work, Lukács felt considerable nostalgia for a lost condition of unity; in his later work, he
believed a new source of unity had been found in the project
of Marxism.

This philosopher and critic was also a political leader and
government figure. But when he did not actually hold office,
he usually lived outside Hungary, in political exile, in embattled relationship to the existing government and certain forms
of Marxism.[5] Despite being a political leader, Lukács felt considerable anxiety about the meaning of Hungarian national
identity, an anxiety that was exacerbated by the use of German and German traditions in Hungarian literature or philos-
ophy.[6] Lukács himself wrote in German.

Lukács claimed that his early background and personal
history had little influence on his writing. It seems more likely
that concepts such as "transcendental homelessness" and
"reification" were connected to his outsider experiences and
came in part from being Jewish by birth—being a member of
the "homeless race" in philosophical traditions, and the essen-
tialized object of anti-Semitism. For many European writers,
especially at the beginning of the twentieth century, the con-
cept of "race" was highly fragmented, politically charged, and
determined by factors not generally considered "racial" in the
United States—language group, political history, religion, and
national origin, for example. (The world has been reminded
of this in the former Yugoslavia and Soviet Union.) Allusions
to the Anglo-Saxons, the Slavs, or Jews as races were common. For writers, like Lukács, who belonged to "races"
deemed exotic but inferior, the urge to slip out of ethnicity
and into some collective European "we" was extremely powerful.[7]

A Jew without religion or heritage; a politician without a

secure national identity; a Marxist censored by many Marxists—Lukács's history of difficulty in fitting comfortably within larger groups is manifest. But so too is the desire for identification. Lukács's "we" hooks up with a pan-European or pan-intellectual community. It affirms the privileges of membership. But it omits what must have been very vivid senses of exclusion. So that while Lukács's writing sounds confident and arouses anxieties in readers, it also and simultaneously masks the writer's potential concerns and insecurities. Both sides of the circuit are energized by the rage to be part of the "we"— to be a cultural insider.

Lukács bears quick comparison on this point to other writers, of whom Dante and T. S. Eliot can serve as examples. During an audacious scene near the beginning of the *Inferno*, Dante has just been ushered by Virgil into Limbo, the anteroom to Hell, where the virtuous pagans are housed. There, amid "a blaze of light that was enclosed in a hemisphere of darkness," he sees a party of four great classical poets and thinkers conversing. The group sees Virgil and Dante and interrupts its conversation to "make a sign of greeting" that marks Dante as "the sixth among those high intelligences."[8] Dante is crowned with laurel even here, just a few pages into his epic *Commedia*. The poet affirms his greatness in advance; his welcoming reception by the prior poets has the force of certainty rather than daydream.

T. S. Eliot, a great admirer of Dante, reproduces the poet's moment with the great masters in his essay "Tradition and the Individual Talent." Eliot was thirty-one when he published this essay, which is riddled with anxious allusions to the question of how a poet can sustain himself after the age of twenty-five. Eliot's answer is establishing rapport with what he calls "the mind of Europe," the mind of "the nation" broadened beyond national boundaries by being linked to the "critical turn of mind" of "the race." Here is Eliot's version of the same incomplete circle that Dante invokes at the beginning of the *Inferno*:

> The historical sense compels a man to write not merely with his own generation in his bones, but with a feeling that the whole of the literature of Europe from Homer and within it the whole of the literature of his own country has a simultaneous existence and composes a simultaneous order. . . . The existing monuments form an ideal order among themselves, which is modified by the introduction of the new (the really new) work of art among them. The existing order is complete before the new work arrives; for the order to persist after the supervention of novelty, the whole order must be, if ever so slightly, altered.[9]

Eliot identifies with the great names of the past as one in an immortal but expandable line of descent. Like Dante and Lukács, Eliot writes as if he has no doubts, no doubts at all, that his poems—and the very essay at hand—are effecting readjustments in the Western tradition.

Yet as for Lukács, even the briefest of biographies shows that the critical "we" in these instances was likely to have masked feelings of doubt and exclusion. Dante was a thirteenth-century Florentine, a believing Christian and a fierce patriot, living in bitter exile at the end of his life and writing his *Commedia,* the work that will justify himself to a world in which neither fellow citizens nor popes could be trusted. Eliot was a twentieth-century American from St. Louis, Missouri, seared by marital unhappiness, beset by religious doubts (though soon to experience conversion), living voluntarily in England, with little acknowledged intellectual identification with the United States.

Even rendered schematically, the life histories of Lukács, Dante, and Eliot have differences from each other and from what was considered normative in their cultures. Those differences would multiply if the descriptions brought other categories to bear, such as class origins, wealth, sexuality, parenthood, and temperament. Their expressed political allegiances varied enormously, spanning a spectrum from revolutionary (Lukács) to conservative (Eliot). Their strongest shared experience was, perhaps, exile from their homelands. Yet in each case, the writer positions himself within a "we" that effaces particularities and affirms identification with a larger body whose common features are relatively bloodless—consisting mostly of maleness, European origin, and education in philosophical traditions. Some might call this unblinking allegiance to what Eliot calls "the historical sense," to the Western tradition in its most abstract form, transcendence—and see it as the proper goal of education. But it is also a shortcut to authority, dishonest in its relationship to existing traditions because it leaves out the personal voice.

In "The Mark of Gender," Monique Wittig says that the personal pronoun, the "I," marks "the pathways and the means of entrance into language" and asserts, in philosophical terms, the subject status of the speaker or writer.[10] Wittig further says that the plural form multiplies the effect of the singular personal pronoun, asserting group identities and goals: "Each new class that fights for power must, to reach its goal, represent its interest as the common interest of all the members of the society" (69).[11] As an affirmation of subject status, the "I" is strategic; the "we" amplifies the same strategy, with a leap into the universal that allows the writer to speak for the culture. And that, I believe, is its special lure for cultural critics.

Yet the "we" I have described so far betrays the spirit of the first person at both levels. It offers the bribe of authority and tradition, and the security of belonging—but at the cost of losing touch with the "I" behind the "we." It establishes false alliances that cover up the writer's sense of isolation or pain. It coerces and assumes the agreement of the "you" it addresses. And it masks the multifaceted complexity of group identities. Critics have been sensitive to how the "we" ignores or demonizes individuals or groups it excludes—no trivial danger.[12] But the inclusive "we" also enacts a politics of repression, in which those who identify with it must surrender crucial aspects of themselves. My resistance to the "we" comes in part from the frustrated desire to think about culture as Dante, Eliot, or Lukács did. But it also comes from a certain contradictory enjoyment of the fact that I cannot. I suspect that my distance from the "we" grew not just from being Italian American but also female, for many of the passages I have quoted suggest that this voice comes most naturally to a man, not a woman—a man who (in Eliot's terms) feels "his generation" in "his bones," whose intellectual fathers welcome adopted sons. Part of my resistance to the "we," part of the reason that I notice it at all, has to do with being outside some of the traditional "we"'s assumptions, most of all its assumption of masculinity.

But I am not, when all is said and done, barred from using the "we" in any definitive way—my education and profession guarantee that, as well as the existence, by 1993, of numerous women's traditions with which to affiliate. In fact, I have used the "we" in my writing (albeit untraditionally).[13] My resistance, even hostility, to the "we" must have additional sources. I believe it to be in part temperamental, having to do with contradictory desires to belong to groups and the fear of being a joiner I have cultivated since adolescence. But the phenomenon is not limited to adolescents. And it has consequences for writing by intellectuals. I do not object to the "we" voice in and of itself. What I object to is the easy slide from "I" to "we" that takes place almost unconsciously—and is often the hidden essence of cultural criticism. This slide can make the "we" function not as a device to link writer and reader, or as a particularized group voice, or even the voice of "the culture," but rather as a covert, and sometimes coercive, universal. I want to slow down that slide to recover the "I" behind the "we."

II

But first I need to come closer to home, to some immediate contexts for me. I never met Dante or Lukács or Eliot. I did meet Lionel Trilling, at least slightly, when I was a graduate student at Columbia University during the seventies. Trilling illustrates with unusual clarity the dynamics of the "we" in "cultural criticism," a term with which his name was synonymous for several decades.[14] People associate the cultural we with Trilling and, when the people are women, they almost always resent it.[15] For me, Trilling remains a touchstone of the "we"—a critical voice I wanted both to emulate and avoid.

In *The Opposing Self* (1955), Trilling says that the "we" reveals a "writer's notion of what constitutes the interesting and the valuable . . . what constitutes 'us'"—and this is a bald statement of the "we"'s exclusionary bent.[16] When he was accused of addressing a changeable "we," but most often the narrow "we" of New York intellectuals, Trilling disagreed, but defined further.[17] Yes, he said, his "we" changes from essay to essay, but it is never narrow. Most often, he said, it refers to "the temper of our age," a temper embodied in New York intellectuals because of the "assiduity" with which this group pursues ideas. Even more strongly, Trilling claimed that this group represented all others: "The structure of our society is such that a class of this kind is bound by organic filaments to groups less culturally fluent that are susceptible to its influence."[18]

For Trilling, the "we" was powerfully, almost infinitely expandable. He advocated a Mandarin or Brahmin system—

other groups being, in Trilling's words, "less culturally fluent"—but not really what he thought of as an exclusionary one. Anyone not part of the intelligentsia was still "organically filamented" with it; anyone could rise from one group to another. His elegant language refers, I believe, to biological origins: people could be born into families that were culturally deprived and yet still learn to speak as intellectuals.[19]

"Organic filamentation" was part of Trilling's belief that universities serve what we might call the "melting pot" project of U.S. culture. Universities, he thought, could teach the huddled masses in the U.S. to breathe freely together: an eminently liberal and democratic ideal. But in presiding over the mechanisms by which "cultural fluency" was achieved, his "we" could seem coercive, as in the following sentences, which are typical of his style:

> *Emma* is more difficult than any of the hard books we admire [Proust or Joyce, for example]
>
> • • • •
>
> If we speak of encyclopedias, there is one actual encyclopedia which we must have in recollection—the great *Encyclopedie* itself.[20]

In the eighties and nineties, the canon has often been linked to a repressive intellectual politics. That view is both right and wrong. For critics like Trilling, the canon was a gatekeeper of sorts—but clearly one thought of as genial and generous. Anyone who took the trouble to read great books would be admitted through the gate; more, anyone willing to take the critic's version of things on provisional faith could be admitted to the "we," could come along with "us" to *Emma* or "the great *Encyclopedie* itself." Belief in the open gate of tradition is one reason some critics have been so hostile toward what they call "canon-busting": these recent tendencies seem to besmirch and threaten a noble, socially useful educational mission.

Ultimately Trilling's view of the canon as the thing that will make culture cohere dovetails with recent critiques: there is no question of the canon coming to the masses; the masses must come to the canon. Still, it's important to catch the open invitation in Trilling's sentences, the way that all readers are welcome to read the texts to which he refers and the way that the reading will suffice. Trilling's sentences present themselves as the Ellis Island of intellectual life, and are the product of an immigrant culture. The canon is like the Statue of Liberty, transforming the huddled masses into an intellectual community.

This assimilationist metaphor cuts to the bone of the politics of the "we" in writing about culture today. As a working-class child whose parents did not go to college, I believe that education gives power. As an undergraduate and graduate student I felt that reading the same books, the great books, will make a culture cohere and help fulfill the desire for seamless community. Even now, as a professor, I find that idea appealing. This faith in books, this hunger for wisdom and harmony to come from books, remains alluring. Yet the model was always utopian, as Trilling's own history reveals.

Thinking of Trilling, I recall immediately certain facts: his immigrant origins; his Jewishness; his embattled status as a young professor at Columbia, which had not previously tenured Jews and told Trilling, when it tried to terminate his contract, that he would be more comfortable somewhere else.[21] I have lots of reasons for empathizing and even identifying with Trilling—though finally I do not. As Russell Jacoby and others have noted, Trilling tended to be "always amazed and appreciative of his good fortune" in the profession—even though he had to negotiate his relationship to "the tradition" and fight, tenaciously, for what he got.[22] All too humanly, once he had crossed over, he identified with the forces that once threatened to exclude him. And he became their defender and embodiment after the student activism of 1968, which accelerated his move from liberalism to reaction.

All his professional life, Trilling tended to separate his "uptown" existence as a Anglophile professor at Columbia from his "downtown" existence writing first for Jewish and then for liberal periodicals.[23] He didn't leave a memoir, or any fully autobiographical writing, and his critical prose rarely contains allusions to his personal history outside his life as a teacher.[24] When I attended his class in the early seventies, near the end of his life, Trilling had taken to reading aloud long passages from his essays and praising them as "elegant" or "well put" without—and this was the curious part—ever identifying them as his own.[25] Looking up at the ceiling and not at his students, reading his own prose aloud, Trilling made himself into the anonymous third person that his "we" always resembled.

It was a puzzling and disturbing performance. Here was this man, so famous, so intellectually powerful—with a wiry elegance of mind that also marked his physical appearance. Yet the man had disappeared into the tradition, a tradition he felt that most of the students before him no longer respected and therefore no longer deserved. His manner was effete and distant—and, finally, both defeated and hostile. His "we" was directed towards the ceiling, not towards his students, sitting there before him. We were the barbarians inside the gates; he wanted none of us. He was a teacher who didn't see us; a role model who would share and be generous with just a chosen few. At the time, I was incompletely aware of what Trilling meant to me; after a lecture or two, I dropped his course and forgot about the possibility of working with him. Now, years later, I can feel both the poignancy and the insult in the scene. I can imagine how pained Trilling must have felt on these occasions. I can also feel my sense of rejection and—even more strongly—my unwillingness to be rejected.

It might make sense at this point to launch a fuller and fiercer attack on Trilling—to use him to the end as a negative model. But I find I simply cannot do that. For Trilling had certain qualities I very much admire. Today his essays can seem old-fashioned and, sometimes, embarrassingly complacent—as when he unblinkingly assumes that culture is, and should be, the sole property of the middle and upper classes.[26] But I still love his definition of culture, which, said Trilling, is not just books, social institutions, and political activity, but the "hum and buzz of implication . . . the things that for good and bad draw the people of a culture together."[27] The allusion to "good and bad" in this definition is one of Trilling's many allusions to the ideal of the critic as "adversarial" to the culture—as an intellectual gadfly, not just a spokesperson or passive supporter—an ideal that continues to motivate today's cultural critics.[28]

Most of all, Trilling at his best was a critic who had a public voice. He had the ability to make educated people care about phenomena like Austen's *Mansfield Park* and the nature of the modern self—and that often years after they had obtained their bachelor's degrees. His best-known and most respected book, *The Liberal Imagination*—a collection of close readings and essays on scholarly topics—sold over 100,000 copies the year it was issued in paperback. Few cultural critics, even today, achieve that level of acceptance among academics and in the general culture, and those who do often encourage the public's skepticism about universities and their mission—a move very different from Trilling's affirmation.[29]

The "we" Trilling used—in the terms he conceived it—may be gone forever. Since the mid-fifties, when Trilling did his best work, things have changed and often through the confluence of circumstances whose full results no one really could have predicted.[30] Today, when awareness of group identities has proliferated, and (from another direction), when all notions of subjectivity are criticized, it might seem best to get rid of the cultural "we" entirely—to simply stop using it.[31] But I don't believe that to be either necessary or desirable. The "I" marks experiences, life histories, emotions, and beliefs. The "we" marks positions, group identifications and allegiances: it can galvanize people for positive goals; it does not have to be ungenerous and pinched. Both the "I" and the "we" operate simultaneously, fluidly, and multiply in a culture. I want the "we" to be an option for critical writers—along with the "I" and criticism's normative third person. But I want a "we" that is different from Trilling's—more open and personal, more fluid and tentative, more aware of differences as well as common ground.

There is no escaping the politics of the we. Again and again, it turns up in public debates. As I finished different versions of this essay, some of the latest examples were multiculturalism and gay rights.[32] There was also an emerging polemic over how, and whether, the U.S. should return to ideas of "community" lost since the 1960s.[33] There will be other examples by the time this essay is read. In these debates, conservatives usually want to preserve some core idea of identity, to circle the wagons and keep "them" out; liberals usually celebrate diversity and difference.

But ultimately the "we" is not just an intellectual issue or a rhetorical one. It affects us all where we live—on our streets, in our communities. "Can't we all get along," said Rodney King, in 1992, during the Los Angeles riots—galvanizing attention at a fearful time. A month later and for a long time after that, King would be a debated, contested figure. But at that moment, before the cameras, he reached out to all Americans. He went to the core of emotion—feelings for all the families whose fathers, sons, wives, or daughters would not be coming home, the shared sense of impotence and sadness.

Differences and shared experiences; the personal and the

communal; what divides and what brings together—the essence of the "we." The "we" is more than a pronoun. Who uses the "we," and how they use it matters. It is a state of mind that establishes who counts and who doesn't, what can or cannot be thought and done.

III

Now I need to come all the way home, to my role as the writer of these essays. Yearning for the "we" but skeptical and even hostile to it, what does it mean to read and write as an Italian American daughter? To me it is axiomatic that Italian American females can and do write in many ways, about many topics, and with varied politics. There is no special identity, no natural sisterhood between Camille Paglia and Sandra M. Gilbert, for example, or Barbara Grizzuti Harrison and Mary Gordon—though all are Italian American females and writers. Still, and above all, writing as an Italian American woman means an awareness of paradox: reading, thinking, writing, finding a voice; imping onto a tradition of active intellectual life which has no branch marked Italian American and female.

I am not alone in seeing the Italian American tradition in stark terms as hostile to its intellectual women. Helen Barolini puts it this way in her Introduction to *The Dream Book,* an anthology of Italian American women's writing: "The Italian woman's soul was in her consecration as core of the family, upholder of its traditions and transmitter of its values." But writing, says Barolini, means breaking away and produces "the sense of being out of line with one's surroundings, not of one's family and not of the world outside the family: an outsider."[34]

When she describes taking her first trip to do research—her first trip ever without parents or husband—Louise De Salvo makes the same point with grim humor:

I come from a family, from a cultural heritage, where women
simply don't go away to do things separately from men. . . .
Women sit around and wait for their men. Or they watch their
children and wait for their men. Or they work very hard and
watch their children and wait for their men. Or they make a
sumptuous meal and they work very hard and watch their children and wait for their men. But they don't go anywhere without their men. Or do anything for themselves alone without
their men. Except complain. About their men and their bad
luck in having been born female.[35]

When Italian American females want professions, books,
learning, independence, writing, they face all the obstacles
women traditionally face, plus one: often, they have to leave
the culture of their childhood. It is clear that men can feel the
book deprivations of Italian American culture too: witness
Mario Puzo in *The Godfather Papers,* who describes how his
decision to be a writer was viewed as madness in Hell's
Kitchen, and he himself as someone who "had gone off his
nut."[36] But intellectual men are more likely to feel and stress
the attractiveness of the culture, its robust plenitude and girth.

When I think of Italian American girlhood, I think above
all of being parceled and bound. I think of the little brides of
Christ, all lined up in identical white veils and dresses, waiting to be confirmed at age thirteen. We file down the aisle of
the church with our adult "sponsors." We walk in silence, careful not to turn our heads or smile at our friends and relatives.
We do not want to stand out—the nuns have told us above all
to avoid doing that. Beneath my veil, I smell the residue of
perm fluid in my hair; I feel stiff crinolines around my hips
and legs. Although I am not to stand out, I feel acutely conscious of being watched—and I hope I look beautiful.

Although no one has made the comparison out loud, confirmation is a dress rehearsal for marriage, and the girls understand it that way, in white dresses and veils, walking down the

aisle. At confirmation, Catholics affirm allegiance to God, their willingness to be "soldiers of Christ." It is a strong, thrilling rhetoric and seems egalitarian, since the boys are there too, dressed in suits and ties, walking down the other aisle in the church. But the aura of equality is a dodge, and the girls know it. The boys will be soldiers; we will be wives. We are really agreeing to be obedient and virtuous—the same values we have always been taught in relationship to males: stay in place, keep quiet, make a gesture of submission at the appropriate moment.

Before confirmation, the priests quizzed and confessed us; now, at the end of the aisle, the bishop will bless us. A row of boys precedes each row of girls to the altar: none of us even questions the order—first male, then female. If they wish, the boys can become the priests and bishops; the girls can only observe that kind of power. The priests and bishops stand in for our male relatives—our fathers, brothers, later husbands, to whom we owe earthly allegiance, rendering unto Caesar.

At the altar, I kneel at the cardinal's feet, receiving his blessing—a hand placed briefly on my head, then a rapid cross made above it. Not a word spoken that is not according to ritual and formula. No speeches or commentaries like those that would impress me years later at Bar or Bat Mitzvahs. Not a sign of individuality, except for the confirmation name, my "sponsor's" name, now ecclesiastically (but not legally) added to my own: Marianna Bernadetta De Marco, Bernadetta being the real name of my "sponsor," whom I have always called Aunt Minnie.

But the new name did not fool me into feeling special on this occasion—and I dropped it almost immediately. Before me, that day in church, there were dozens of girls. After me, there were also dozens—all wearing identical veils and white dresses. Even our brand-new garter belts and stockings—the ball and chain of womanhood—were standard department store issue. I wanted to be done with that kind of femininity, that kind of conformity. With confirmation behind me, I was ready to make my move.

THE DAY BEFORE CONFIRMATION, as the Church required, I made confession. As the priest shut the gate that separated my face from his, I said to myself: Well, that's that; after tomorrow I won't be back. I had made my last confession. I sauntered out to the porch of the church and announced my resolution to my friends, who doubted I would make it stick. "What about your parents?" some of them said. But I was sure I could handle them. "What about getting married?" my friend Connie asked triumphantly. "Maybe I won't get married," I said, shocking them all—then, hedging my bets, "or maybe I'll have a civil ceremony."

I kept my vow. I had that civil ceremony. I've never been back to confession. I returned to that church only for one uncle's funeral, then another's, and then, just last year, for my father's. It wasn't the church that drew me. It was the family, the way that tradition expresses itself most for Italian Americans. Still, recently, I have become aware of a certain feeling beneath my bravado for what I cast away: not the church, but the belonging, not the submission, but the participation in ceremony and ritual. Richard Rodriquez has called Catholics the people of the "we"—with an instinct and training for effacing the self and embracing group emotion. I have to confess: it is true, even years after I had willed something different.

When Italian American daughters rebel, their "I-ness" comes through loud and strong—but so too does their remembrance of the "we." They feel the lure of family and community—the thrill of self-sacrifice. The "I" is a heady release conflicted by a potent nostalgia. I want the "I" with its hunger for difference and freedom. But I want the "I" to linger along with the "we"—to be part, somehow, of our collective memory.

Notes

1. Georg Lukács, *History and Class Consciousness: Studies in Marxist Dialectics*, trans. Rodney Livingstone (Cambridge, Mass.: MIT Press), 100.

Lukács's original German text uses "man" and "wir" ("man"/"one" and "we") interchangeably. In German, this specific passage uses "man" where the "we" appears in translation; still, the translator is entirely true to the passage in using the English "we." In fact, many other passages in the German essay use the "wir" voice throughout or in tight alternation with the German "man." When I refer below to Lukács's "we," I include both actual uses of the "wir" and equivalents like the universal "man" in this passage.

After this note, the essay below does not attempt to take account of how the "we" form functions in different languages. Among the complications would be the reflexive forms typical of certain languages and the connotations of different forms of address, neither of which is important in English. Another factor would be whether a language is rich in pronouns (like Japanese) or poor in pronouns (like English). For reflections on the "we" in different languages, see Emile Benveniste, *History of General Linguistics*, trans. Mary Elizabeth Meek (Coral Gables, Fla.: University of Florida Press, 1971); and Monique Wittig, "The Mark of Gender," in *The Poetics of Gender*, ed. Nancy K. Miller (New York: Columbia University Press, 1986), 63–74.

2. The encroachment of "things" on people is an outstanding theme in the late Dickens, for example, in *Our Mutual Friend*. In the twentieth century, D. H. Lawrence continues to explore the theme obsessively. Lukács's essay is helpful in naming and understanding the phenomena their fictions and other modernist documents record.

3. See Lee Congdon, *The Young Lukács* (Chapel Hill: University of North Carolina Press, 1983) for biographical information. See also Istvan Eorsi, ed., *Georg Lukács, Record of a Life* (London: Verso, 1983), a set of interviews with Lukács himself. A rich pictorial record of the life is available in Eva Fekete and Eva Karadi, eds., *Gyorgy Lukács: His Life in Pictures and Documents* (Budapest: Corvina Kiado, 1981).

4. Georg Lukács, *The Theory of the Novel*, trans. Anna Bostock (Cambridge, Mass.: MIT Press, 1971). Originally published, in German, in 1920.

5. Lukács was Minister of Culture in 1956, at the time of the failed Hungarian Revolution. Along With Imre Nagy, who led the Hungarian government, Lukács was interned in Romania for many years—his most notorious period of exile. Many Hungarians failed to survive similar exiles. Although Lukács was invited throughout these years to denounce Nagy (with whom Lukács had often disagreed in public statements), he refused to do so. Lukács was denied Communist Party membership from 1957–67, and even after 1967 was regarded as a "chief ideological risk." His growing international reputation in the seventies protected him near the end of his life. The interviews in *Georg Lukács: A Record of a Life* detail the Romanian exile and other periods of exile in Vienna, Berlin, and the Soviet Union.

6. See Congdon, *The Young Lukács*, 8–9.

7. I have in mind here writers such as Henry M. Stanley, Joseph Conrad, Bronislaw Malinowski, and Sigmund Freud. Stanley was a Welshman who claimed he was an American from the South and idealized in his writing the racial type of the Anglo-Saxon; Conrad and Malinowski were Slavic Poles who aspired to being part of an English-speaking "us"; Freud was an Austrian Jew who idealized the model of the Roman citizen. I discuss each of these figures and their relationship to a European "we" in *Gone Primitive: Savage Intellects, Modern Lives* (Chicago: University of Chicago Press, 1990).

8. Dante Alighieri, *Inferno*, trans. John D. Sinclair (New York: Oxford University Press, 1961), 63.

9. T. S. Eliot, "Tradition and the Individual Talent" (1919), in *The Selected Prose of T. S. Eliot*, ed. Frank Kermode (New York: Harcourt, Brace, Jovanovich, 1975), 38.

10. Wittig, "The Mark of Gender," 65.

11. Wittig is actually discussing at this point her use of *elles* in *Les Guérillières*, a plural third-person feminine that does not exist in English. Her point remains applicable to the first-person plural in English.

12. See especially Edward Said, *Orientalism* (New York: Pantheon, 1978).

13. In *Gone Primitive*, I summarize general ideas about "the primitive" using the "we" voice. I call attention to the levels of resistance statements made in this voice are likely to produce in certain readers.

14. The terms Cultural Criticism and Cultural Studies are often used as synonyms. The term Cultural Studies originated in British Left politics and hence is often associated with the Left—but this is by no means always the case in this country. At an earlier point, Cultural Criticism would have confined itself to "high" and Cultural Studies to "mass" or "popular" culture. That distinction is no longer fully viable.

15. See Carolyn Heilbrun, "Presidential Address," *PMLA*, 99:4 (May 1984), 408. Heilbrun's story has an ambiguous ending: in 1992, she resigned from Columbia, citing its old-boy mentality and her frustration as a feminist (see Anne Matthews, "Rage in a Tenured Position," *New York Times Magazine*, November 8, 1992, 46–47, 75, 83. See also Nancy Miller, "Decades," *Writing Cultural Criticism*, ed. Marianna Torgovnick, special issue of *SAQ*, Winter 1992. A female character in the recent film *Metropolitan* argues with a man who insists on quoting from an essay in which Trilling uses the "we."

16. Lionel Trilling, *The Opposing Self: Nine Essays in Criticism* (New York: Viking Press, 1955), ix.

17. See "Preoccupations of a Critic," *Times Literary Supplement*, August 26, 1955, 492; and Graham Hough, "'We' and Lionel Trilling," *Listener 75* (1955), 760. Hough found Trilling's we "monotonously apocalyptic."

18. Lionel Trilling, *Beyond Culture* (New York: Viking Press, 1965), ix–xi.

19. Trilling himself was born into a middle-class family; he was much aware of how most Jewish intellectuals rose from working to middle class. See Diana Trilling, *The Beginning of the Journey: The Marriage of Diana and Lionel Trilling* (New York: Harcourt, Brace and Co., 1993).

20. The quotations are from *Beyond Culture*, 52, 36.

21. For two accounts of these matters, see Diana Trilling, "Lionel Trilling, A Jew at Columbia," *Commentary* 67 (March 1979) 3:44; and Russell Jacoby, *The Last Intellectuals: American Culture in the Age of Academe* (New York: Farrar, Straus and Giroux, 1987).

22. Jacoby, 84.

23. See Mark Krupnick, *Lional Trilling and the Fate of Cultural Criticism* (Evanston: Northwestern University Press, 1986).

24. Trilling's single novel, *The Middle of the Journey* (1947; New

York: Harcourt, Brace, Jovanovich, 1980) does contain covert autobiographical references.

25. As a graduate student, I recognized his prose and some of the specific essays from which he read; I suspect the undergraduates were baffled by this aspect of his classes.

26. For example: "In a complex culture there are, as I say, many different systems of manners and since I cannot talk about them all, I shall select the manners and attitude towards manners of the literate, reading, responsible middle class people who are ourselves" ("Manners, Morals, and the Novel," in *The Liberal Imagination* [New York: Viking, 1950], 207). This essay was originally a lecture delivered to a largely middle-class group—a partial excuse. And Trilling is of course right that culture was, and continues to be, largely associated with the middle classes and above. It is only his lack of reflection on this state of affairs, as in his use of the word *responsible* above, that seems insufficiently thoughtful.

27. "Manners, Morals, and the Novel," 206–7. This view of culture, which is widely shared by critics of the novel, may explain why such critics often also write cultural criticism,

28. The idea derives from Matthew Arnold's *Culture and Anarchy;* Arnold wanted intellectuals to leaven Philistine culture. Edward Said articulates a later version of the same idea, using the terms "secular criticism" and "oppositional criticism" in *The World, the Text, and the Critic* (Cambridge, Mass.: Harvard University Press, 1983).

29. I think especially of Alan Bloom's *The Closing of the American Mind: How Higher Education Has Failed Democracy and Impoverished the Souls of Today's Students* (New York: Simon and Schuster, 1987).

30. Among them would be the wide availability of scholarships and fellowships after Sputnik; the Civil Rights movement; feminism; the gay rights movement; awareness that the "melting pot" has not worked for racial minorities; and the increased influence of certain ethnic groups, like my own group, the Italian Americans.

31. The unity and coherence of "the subject position" have been attacked by various forms of poststructuralist thought as "essentialist." Many feminists and African American scholars disagree, though they otherwise belong to forms of poststructuralism. These critics argue for the strategic necessity of retaining the subject position in discourse. See, for example, Nancy Hartsock, "Rethinking Mod-

ernism," *Cultural Critique* 7 (Fall 1987), 187–206 and Henry Louis Gates, Jr., "The Master's Pieces: On Canon Formation and the African-American Tradition," in *The Politics of Liberal Education,* eds. Darryl J. Gless and Barbara Herrnstein Smith, *SAQ* 89:1 (Winter 1990). Defense of the discursive subject can also be said to assume that no writing (even writing in the third person) can really avoid "the subject position"—so that the poststructuralist point can be both conceded and seen as having no consequences.

The literature on this issue is extensive. See also Gayatri Chakravorty Spivak, "French Feminism in an International Frame," *Yale French Studies,* no. 62 (1981); and Paul Smith, *Discerning the Subject,* Theory and History of Literature v. 55 (Minneapolis: University of Minnesota Press, 1988). Smith makes a useful distinction between the word *agent* and the word *subject.* He wants to redeem the idea of the acting or writing being who claims no absolute power on the world or absolute coherence of being. See also Diana Fuss, *Essentially Speaking* (New York: Routledge, 1989).

32. The original version of this essay, published in *SAQ* (Winter 1991) discussed the multiculturalism debate extensively.

33. This debate crossed racial lines but took especially interesting forms among African Americans, many of whom perceived the segregation previous to the sixties as having been attended by communal structures which were in fact more viable than those of the present day.

34. Helen Barolini, *The Dream Book: An Anthology of Writings by Italian American Women* (New York: Schocken, 1985), 12, 19.

35. Louise De Salvo, from "Portrait of the *Puttana* as a Middle-Aged Woolf Scholar," in Helen Barolini, ed., *The Dream Book,* 94.

36. Mario Puzo, *The Godfather Papers and Other Confessions* (New York: Fawcett, 1972), 15.

Epilogue

Crossing Back

FOR MY FATHER, SALVATORE DE MARCO, SR. 1912–1992

I

When I was a child, I thought of my father as connected to the larger world—the glittering "City." Every day, my tall, slim father dressed in a dark suit and tie, combed his brown hair with a pronounced part to the side, groomed his thin Don Ameche moustache and headed for "the City"—a Rudolph Valentino look-alike, very Italian. My father knew "the City" and it was a point of pride for him; the "King of New York," my husband called him recently. My father was born in Manhattan, on the Lower East Side, and the New York of his youth was his private heartland. He boasted about having been rough in school and being kicked out in the eighth grade after a fight in which his nose was broken into an exaggerated Roman beak. He would tell again and again how he was expelled; bored with the story, my mother would murmur with vague disapproval, "Oh yeah, a tough guy."

For most of the years I was growing up, my father had a job that put him in touch with "the City." He was a messenger for a large bank—First National City, now Citibank; actually, he was what was called an armed guard, delivering stocks, bonds, and cash from office to office and for a while collecting payments in Harlem with a black partner he liked named Oscar Joseph. Later, he worked in the mail room of an insurance company and he liked this job too. But my father loved best his bank job, and the gun he carried as an armed messenger added a certain jauntiness to his image.

At the bank, the city was his beat. It was the equivalent of the police route he always coveted but couldn't get. My father was six feet tall—unusual among second-generation Sicilian Americans—but he was too thin for his height to pass the physical examination for the Police Department. He took the physical three times; it was part of the family lore that he gulped malteds several times a day before the last examination. But although he always had a hearty appetite, he just couldn't gain enough weight—and it was a profound disappointment. All his life, my father would say of certain acquaintances, with admiration and a kind of hush in his voice, "He's a cop." He kept track of raises in policemen's pay scales; he loved detective shows on T.V. I think he always felt he had missed out on a certain level of excitement, missed out as well on the financial security of being a policeman for the city.

Still, at the bank, Manhattan was his beat and he took personal responsibility for knowing it. My father could reel off the exact location of everything—hotels, movie theaters, even stores and restaurants. He knew the subway and bus routes by heart. He never wanted to leave New York and would tell people again and again when he visited us in North Carolina that he was a New Yorker and that outside of New York everything was "boring." Later in life, after he had retired and stopped going into Manhattan regularly, one of his most annoying habits was continuing to give directions to places that had changed, especially driving directions, since he never drove.

But when I was young, my father's intimacy with the city was his special charm. He took me on excursions that must have been on his vacations, since my mother was never there and was probably working. We went to out-of-the-way museums, like the Museum of the City of New York; to zoos and parks for sledding; to Wall Street (where he worked). To Radio City Music Hall or the old Roxy (these with my mother) every birthday, to see the movie and stage shows. These were places that made me feel the pulse of life beyond Brooklyn—and my father was, at first, the key.

He also introduced me to the world of reading. Until he needed glasses, my father was an avid reader. He would pass along the newspaper every day after work and sometimes paperbacks he got from friends. Once, via Oscar Joseph, I got the autobiography of Althea Gibson, an African American female tennis player. It was typical of my father that he was friendly towards blacks in a general way, despite sharing some of the prejudices of our neighborhood: without really thinking about it, he taught me tolerance by little things like his stories about his buddy Oscar Joseph and the book about Gibson. But my father always claimed he could not read using glasses— and so he simply stopped reading once and for all when he was in his fifties and had to use them. In later years, I would sometimes buy him books I thought he might like about the Mafia or mysteries but he never read them—because of the glasses.

My father smoked exactly a pack a day between the ages of ten and sixty and then gave up cigarettes cold turkey—as firmly and definitely as he gave up reading. He also never ate cake after dinner, just at breakfast, and never used more than one slice of cold cuts in his sandwiches. He was a man with many rules—some of them nonsensical—which he would proclaim repeatedly as simple matters of fact: "Nope. I don't eat cake at night" or "That's right, just one slice of provolone." As he aged, I saw the rigidity in his life but forgot the younger man, the reader, the adventurer who took me all over town. I needed to forget in order to become myself. For if adolescents need rebellion, female adolescents in Bensonhurst need it even more. Now I am free to remember.

II

My father, who always liked above all things to walk, got lung cancer. Within two months of the diagnosis, he could only walk a half block at a time. On a good day—a very good day— he walked five short blocks and felt euphoric. All his life he had been prone to exaggerate minor illnesses. After he retired, he paced the floor, restlessly, and jingled change in his pockets. He lost interest in almost everything but a few weekly T.V. shows. He became irritable over nothing. I thought he might fall apart at the lung cancer. Instead, he pulled together. Now that he had something real to worry about, he was able to act brave. Bringing up the subject of a living will and signing one frankly. "I don't want to be a guinea pig," he said. "You have to help me get the words right"—but his own words were pretty good. He made calls to see if any social agency would provide help for him and my mother. Being brave. Taking charge.

In the months after I learned he had lung cancer, I was bombarded with memories. Once, when I was about five, my father was reading the *Daily News*. On the front page was a picture of Marilyn Monroe during her marriage to Joe DiMaggio. The headline was about a miscarriage (not, I think, her first). "What a shame," my father said. "Such a beautiful woman, so famous, and she just can't do what a woman is supposed to do." The very things that would so frustrate me about Italian Americans were all there in his remark—the narrow aspirations for women, the expectation that they must bear children, the disregard for things other than family—but at the time I didn't have a single feminist hackle to raise and I'm sure as sure that this remark lodged firmly in my subconscious.

So firmly that I connect this memory seamlessly with one from twenty years later, sitting with my father on my front porch the week my own baby died. He didn't know that I felt I had failed, just like Marilyn. Without a hint of the bravado that might accompany such a remark, just matter of factly, my father said, "It should have been me instead of that baby. I would have been happy to die instead." These were his only words to me on the subject, ever, and somehow they were enough since I knew what he meant. A pragmatic man, he wanted to keep the generations straight and spare me improper pain: he should have died, not the baby.

My other, strongest, memory of my father comes from when I was about ten. He had just gotten off the phone with his brother, talking about his niece, my cousin Marion, much older than me and the mother of my playmate Patricia. Marion had cancer. They weren't sure yet how bad. "It's bad," my father said to my mother, as he hung up the phone. "It's spread through her body. She's going to die." His voice croaked, his eyes were red, and there were tears beginning to roll down his face. Then he wiped his eyes heartily with a handkerchief, and that was all. Marion was his favorite niece—fat and always jolly. But there was no helping a bad situation, and no privacy for expressing grief in our small apartment. I think my father didn't want to scare me, who was watching. But it did scare me—especially since, after Marion died, he sometimes accidentally called me by her name, so close to mine, a momentary confusion that I understand now, when I sometimes call one daughter by the other's name. "Oh, Mom!" they say, exasperated. But when my father called me Marion it made me shiver—his calling me by my dead cousin's name.

There's a way to see these memories as about Italian American contempt for females. My father telling me early that women were valuable only as reproducers. My father crying at my female cousin's death but not wanting to make too big a deal of it. My father confusing my name with his niece's. But these readings would be wrong.

My father was not a philosophical man, not able to or even interested in expressing what he felt. Nor was he an especially sensitive or demonstrable man, emotionally. He was a family man, devoted to custom because in his experience custom was what kept families going. People had children because people loved their children and took care of them: nothing in life was more basic than that to my father. You didn't make a big deal of things or fall apart because that would make it harder to keep going: that was basic too. Even as a child, I understood the way he reacted to Marilyn, Marion, and me, Marianna, to show that I was important to him, that my mother's life would have been—from his point of view, and hers—incomplete without my being born. My mother was thirty when she married and thirty-six when she had me: a career woman's pattern today. But back then she had no career and was in danger of spending her life as a maiden aunt, caring for her sister's family. My father had saved her from what would have been in his terms a "waste," even a "disgrace." So he was not devaluing females; he was valuing them in the way he knew best.

In fact, my father loved his female relatives intensely. He adored his mother, who lived with my parents after their marriage and died a few months before I was born and given her name. In her last illness, some kind of pneumonia, he tried to give her mouth-to-mouth resuscitation when she stopped breathing. He wondered aloud, sometimes, if he had killed her; my mother always said quickly, "No, don't think it. She was dead already." He was extremely close to his sister, Minnie, visiting her several times every week until she died in 1982.

My father was unusual among Italian men in that he was always involved with running the house. He did housework—perhaps because my mother worked, perhaps because he liked it, but I suspect because he remembered his own mother as tired. Each time, he would draw the blinds and instruct us not to tell the neighbors that he was ironing, doing the dishes, whatever it happened to be. I didn't understand his concern, since it didn't seem shameful to me that a man should do chores. I can still see him wearing what we agreed to call my mother's aprons or, more often, a dish towel tucked into his belt. When he was young, he was a painter and also finished furniture (breathing every day, I realize now, fumes and asbestos); so he did traditional men's work too, like painting and putting up wallpaper. Until he was into his seventies, he could be counted on to do repairs well—it was part of his public image. After that, he became a little obsessive about the details, scrubbing pots for hours (his tongue protruding as it always did when he concentrated) and he sometimes broke what he tried to fix.

LOOKING BACK, PUTTING TOGETHER the pieces, I understand my father to have been my ally in crossing Ocean Parkway. He was pulling for me underneath—though not always and not uniformly. He was proud of my bookishness and sensitivity. But he was an Italian American male—so he worried about them too. At times, he could be macho and even cruel in attempts to "toughen me up" and teach me to follow orders. Some of what I learned was useful later in life; but even now I feel ambivalent about the lessons.

Once, for example, when I was about five, I cried hard at a Jerry Lewis skit on T.V. and my father banished me in a rage from the living room. In the skit, Jerry was a poor kid in a rich community who had worked hard all summer to buy a lottery ticket for a bicycle; he won, but couldn't make it through the crowd in time to claim his prize. I still think it wasn't funny, it was sad—though I probably overreacted. My father couldn't understand why I would cry over something that happened on T.V. Television was background noise or entertainment and neither he nor my mother would ever take it to heart. My father got mad and wouldn't let me watch television for a week until I learned to "control myself and not spoil things for other people."

Similar things happened when I just couldn't sit at the table when a Sicilian delicacy called what sounded like "capuzeddu" (*capozella*) was served—a whole, baked sheep's head with gaping eyes and exposed larynx. "She's too soft; she's got to learn," he would say to my mother—and he'd make me eat in the bathroom, sitting on the washing machine. At first, being sent off alone made me feel sad and rejected; I wanted to control myself, to be part of the family circle. But gradually something else took shape—a feeling of pride in being different. At school, teachers praised me for empathizing with books and having strong opinions; I was appointed "school librarian," so that I could spend several hours each day alone, reading or doing whatever I wanted. I think I came to associate being on my own with being special. So by the time I was ten or eleven, I began to rather like these scenes of banishment at home.

At other times, my father could be patient and supportive. When I was put ahead from second to third grade in the middle of the school year, he sat with me for hours, teaching me cursive writing, making the transition work. "A Philadelphia lawyer!" he would joke when I said something clever. He was hostile to the Church for reasons he never revealed—and that made it easier for me to break away when I was fourteen. Once he had started me on going to "the City," I kept going and I always had money for things like movies and plays. I suspect now, in retrospect, that these kinds of luxuries were my father's doing, just as it was my mother who provided extra money for clothes.

My mother sewed dresses in a factory near our apartment and only went to Manhattan for Radio City to see the shows or, sometimes, to shop with me. She was smart and strong, the kind of woman who could have been a CEO in a different life. But if she had been making decisions about me alone I suspect I would have been confined more to "the neighborhood." My father did not dream wild dreams but he definitely saw me in the world of "the City." He wavered just enough in his opposition to my ambitions (letting me go to college, for example, but not out of town) so that while I did not exactly get what I wanted, I got what I would need.

III

During my father's illness my visits to Bensonhurst grew more frequent. I saw different sides of the neighborhood from those I saw as a child and teenager. My father had always been faithful in visiting people in hospitals or attending funerals. This is an important part of Italian American life and one reason why my father was so familiar with sickness and death—much more so than I am, his Americanized daughter. Now people returned the "respect" he had shown. The neighbors didn't desert my parents or avert their eyes politely. People visited, some every day, some more than once a day. Food arrived. Connie next door delivered grapefruits, apples, eggs, bread, cakes. She offered the extra room in her apartment if I needed to stay overnight. Sometimes I did stay, surrounded by statues of the Virgin Mary and Saint Teresa, and by numerous pictures of Il Papa, Pope Paul. The barber across the street volunteered his services for both parents. The community drew together, as it always has done best, in times of trouble.

Back in Bensonhurst, I felt observed and shut in, as usual.

But there was something else taking shape as I contrasted the neighborhood's reaction to my father's illness with the college town where I had last experienced grief: there was no embarrassment here, no shunning. Some of the aloofness and reserve I had cultivated towards the neighbors began to change. I was grateful for their help, willing to listen politely to their stories in exchange, giving the ritual kisses and hugs sincerely.

In the same way, I felt close to my brother in a way I had not for years, even decades, as our politics and ways of life grew apart. Again and again, I was surprised at how little we had to say to understand what the other was thinking—and at how much we thought alike. Once, when my father suddenly seemed worse, I asked my brother if I should come to New York immediately. "I can't say, Marianna," he responded. "That's for you to decide." My parents and brother had always been bossy. So while it sounds like a small thing, this comment was golden.

MY FATHER HUNG ON TO LIFE, tenaciously. His fingers clawed the blanket, searching for texture. He concentrated, hard, at hearing conversations from the rooms adjacent to the bedroom, where he was now confined. He talked over, again and again, every detail of where things should be placed in his sickroom—the bed, the clock, his eyeglasses. He was proud of lucid moments when he recognized everyone and everything clearly and could participate in conversation. I was proud too that he retained minutes of lucidity until the end—eating some breakfast and talking to his nurse the very day he died.

More and more, his body gave way on an alert mind. Teeth getting loose; limbs stick-like; jaw swollen grotesquely with a new cancer. A merciless disease that extracted every ounce of strength from my father, still struggling, still brave. And I can't say that there was not some quality of life until the very end: enjoyment of the visits, of the food, of the holidays, even, though it's not clear at all that one day was very different from another. On one visit, I bought a portable television for the bedroom, distressed at the silence in which my father spent his days and nights—so different from the radio and television noise he had always seemed to like. I had always hated the soundtracks of the police shows he preferred, but now I flipped eagerly through the channels, glad when I found one with the right jarring and staccato notes. On that visit, my next to last, my father seemed to be permanently bedridden. I was surprised the next week when he was up once more and I heard him over the phone joking with his visiting nurse at the kitchen table. "It often happens," the nurse said when I called the hospice; "We don't know why but some people get a burst of energy before they go back to bed for good."

As he neared death, he didn't pay attention to petty things—the rules about cake, the glasses, the TV. When he was not lucid he talked to himself, or perhaps (as he made caressing gestures) to his dead mother or sister. When he was alert, my father talked directly about his illness, his coming death. He wanted no nonsense and got none. "I always thought of myself as a tough guy," my father said, "but I'm sure scared now." Near the end, when I asked whether he wanted me to keep talking or just to be silent, he said, "Really, what is there to say?" So I stayed quiet. The day before he died, he said, "This is too much now." So I was glad when it stopped.

IV

At the funeral, it was my father's jolliness people remembered—his sense of humor, his participation in life. Funerals are like résumés—only the good survives—but it pleased me to hear these things from family and my parents' friends.

I had dreaded the Italian funeral, even before I knew it

would fall on New Year's Eve, then New Year's Day, cold and windy. Lots of people were away for the holidays and could not be reached; to my other fears was added the fear that too few people would come. Still, people did come, drifting in and out—relatives (some of whom I had never met), people from the Senior Citizens' Center, neighbors alone or in groups of two and three—talking, remembering, even laughing. Some of them had known my father for fifty, even seventy or more years, and I heard about him as a boy, a teenager, a young man.

The number of flowers in the room grew and grew as the contributions of friends and neighbors arrived. The stands erected for mass cards began to fill. We reached a decent number of visitors, flowers, and cards and I began to feel better. I thought of the irony: this man, who never went to church, will have many masses. I, who thought the cards and flowers meaningless, am keeping tabs.

Before my father died, my mother talked about how she wanted to give the money people might spend on flowers to the hospice that cared for my father near the end. Then, the day he died, she amazed me by reciting a list of flower arrangements she wanted me to order—specific, with names, colors, and sizes: a "Bleeding Heart" for her, three feet across and all made of roses; a carnation "Rosary" for the grandchildren, to hang in the coffin. This woman, who would walk miles to save a dollar on a can of coffee, spent over a thousand dollars on flowers. My brother and I followed her orders unthinkingly. But even we were surprised by the lavishness of the "Gate of Paradise" she had ordered for us. Over five hundred dollars of orchids, roses, and lilies densely woven in a six-foot arch—a real fantasy, "what children give their parents." In the funeral home, looking for hours at these flowers, I thought about how much more useful the money would have been at the hospice; later, we made a contribution in my father's name. But I cannot deny it, I was comforted by the flowers and the funeral cards—so wasteful but so necessary for the occasion.

At first, I found the traditional Italian funeral creepy: people swooping in, making my mother tell the story of the last weeks again and again, making her cry, sometimes outdoing her themselves in tears and drama. Then, everybody settled in. There were fewer new arrivals, and fewer scenes. We were, as is the Italian custom, sitting and keeping watch over the body in the open coffin. My father's body became a comfortable presence in the room. He was wearing a new suit (my mother's preference), and he had been made up skillfully so that he looked healthy and years younger. By the end of the second day, the day before the burial, looking at him, I even wondered why he had to die, though that had been so vivid just days before in the hospice, as he struggled painfully for air.

The familiar rhythms of Italian gossip got going. The funeral "home" is, or so the relatives whispered, favored by the Mafia. Signing some papers, I looked up to see a man with a face so coldblooded and heartless—pocked, stretched, and rubbery like old silly putty, like a cartoon gangster—that it took my breath away. He was wearing a long leather coat, an expensive suit, and gold and diamond rings on every finger. A mafioso, or so it seemed, who became a family joke for the rest of the funeral. I never thought that I identified with the Mafia, or, rather, with Italian Americans' fascination with the Mafia—yet here I was, joining in. It was a bond with my family and my father.

When I was a child I suspected that my missing paternal grandfather, a union organizer for barbers, had had Mafia connections. Then, when I was married and deemed ready for such news, I was told he had been a bad husband, a womanizer, and that was why he was missing from my family's life.

My father had stood up for my grandmother, rebelled against his father, and his father had left the house. It turns out I was right as a child—even though what I was told later on was also true. During the funeral, my brother recalled how my father always said that Lucky Luciano had been his godfather. Among Sicilians, so celebrated a godfather is a real distinction—and no accident. Although he was not a mafioso, my father's father must have needed to have, at the very least, the connivance of the Mafia to run his union. He must have done certain favors and handled himself in a way that won Luciano's "respect." I understand now my father's tacit pride in the Mafia, though the family has been out of the business for two generations and he himself always wanted to be a policeman.

The last stop before the cemetery at an Italian funeral is the church, and here too there were surprises. I had not been in church for years and there were many changes. The priest went about his business energetically and impressively. He minced no words: if we are believing Catholics, there can be no absolute sadness in the face of death. He wafted his incense, controlled his altar. It was an impersonal service, as is typical of Catholic masses. Nothing was said about my father but his name; no space was provided for eulogies, so the one my husband wrote stayed in his pocket unread. Then—I realized too late—the priest offered communion. The entire neighborhood rose and moved to the altar. So did my mother and my brother, although my brother (I could tell from his face and the way he held his body) expected just to escort her to the altar, not to take communion himself.

I had not been to confession, had not fasted, was in a state of mortal sin. I remembered all the warnings of the nuns from my childhood, and feared committing blasphemy at my father's funeral. I stayed seated. So did my husband and daughters, who are not Catholic. I thought it would be a bad moment, but no one, not even the neighbors, seemed to mind.

The priest handed my brother a host, unexpectedly. His face showed confused feelings; then he swallowed it, glaring at me to say absolutely nothing. After mass, people told me that now they decide whether they are ready to take communion—no confession or fasting are needed. I was back in Bensonhurst, and making peace; but I no longer knew all the rules.

V

When a parent dies, you are freed from images of the last few years, from the physical form in which you knew them then. Until a few months before he died, my father was a handsome man of eighty, with abundant silver hair still mixed with black, tall and slim and elegant. His hair would jut forward over his forehead while he worked, making him look almost boyish. He had relatively few wrinkles. The only real signs of his advanced age were his thick glasses and an occasional wobble from an inner ear condition. He was always neatly dressed and never really informal. He looked odd in shorts, which he wore only at the beach. When he lacked a tie or jacket, he often wore a vest or cardigan. He always wore polished or suede shoes, never sneakers, even to take his long daily walks.

But now, in my imagination, my father has floated free of the physical images from his last years. He is the dark-haired, slim man (almost always wearing a dark suit) from the photographs. My father on the subway, holding the straps, teaching me the ropes of going into "the City." My father flying kites at my cousin's country house, helping me chase a kite down a road for miles and miles. I remember still how that kite looked, finally trapped in some telephone wires, as we turned and walked away. I remember the gold tooth he hasn't had since his late fifties, when he got false teeth. There it is in my mind. It's as much a part of my father now as anything else. Then, as I am waking up one morning, I see my eighty-year-old father on the inside of my eyelids—his beaked nose, his thin moustache, his crooked smile. He starts to speak, but it's too late—I'm fully awake. It's so vivid that I need a few seconds to remind myself that he is recently dead.

When a parent dies, you also cross from one state to another. All my life I have defined myself by rebellion against Bensonhurst. But the grounds for rebellion are running out.

Acknowledgments

This book fulfills a long-term ambition to write a collection of essays linked in theme and conception. It includes pieces that are near to my heart, some of which were key forms of emotional exploration and expression.

Several of the essays might not have been written without the example and inspiration of the members of my writing group: Alice Kaplan, Jane Tompkins, and Cathy N. Davidson. Each of these friends has experimented with memoir and produced distinctive results. About half of the pieces in this collection were my part in this group process. I thank my group for: encouraging me in new modes of writing, arguing with me when I was wrong, making me rewrite portions of these essays (sometimes whole essays) time after time—and being willing to read them yet again.

Three other friends provided support and wonderful insights as I neared the end of the writing: Julie Tetel, Elaine Showalter, and Joyce Carol Oates. Elaine Showalter's belief in my work gave me a semester at Princeton University, during which I wrote or rewrote some of these essays. That semester also provided the occasion to spend time in and around New York, with friends and family, and to reassess my relationship to the past. When I was wrestling with the question of how (and whether) to finish "Crossing Back," these women gave generously of their time. Joyce Carol Oates gave what proved to be valuable tips about patience and characterization.

Numerous other people have been helpful in other ways. Morris Dickstein gave me the occasion to finish my essay on Bensonhurst; later he read early versions of the essays on Ocean Parkway and Camille Paglia. Without the strong response I received to "Bensonhurst," I do not know whether some of the later essays would ever have been written. Helen Barolini and Barbara Herrnstein Smith were among those who provided that encouraging response. Anjelika Bammer gave me the occasion to expand the first pages of "Slasher Stories" into a full-fledged essay; the expansion took me places I never expected to go. Frank Lentricchia commissioned the essay on *The Godfather* and the special issue in which "The Politics of the 'We'" first appeared; he and Melissa Lentricchia made excellent suggestions for revision. Carol McGuirk, a friend and former colleague, and Rosa Blitzer Oppenheim—my oldest friend from Bensonhurst—read several essays, helped me remember important things, and kept me honest.

Geri Thoma skillfully placed the book. Susan Ryman, David Lange, and Hugh Stevens provided technical advice. Alan Thomas made a careful (and tough) reading of a much earlier draft of the manuscript which led to a thorough reshaping; then he gave scrupulous and loving attention to the present version. Rachel Brownstein and Anthony Appiah made important suggestions which helped shaped the whole.

Stuart Torgovnick believed in the book from its inception and patiently read and reread versions of its essays. He never questioned my right to probe the past—and I thank him for his remarkable generosity. Only the irruption of death into our family has cheated him of the dedication of this volume, which his time and patience amply deserve.

My daughters, Kate and Elizabeth, were much on my mind as I wrote *Crossing Ocean Parkway*. They are old enough now so that I hope I have not violated their privacy when I mention them. My love for them was an important motivation for the project: I hope especially that they will feel that when they read the essays on their brother and grandfather. Kate neared fourteen as this volume went to press: had she gotten there much earlier, it would have been harder to access the feelings of my own adolescence and I doubt the volume could have been written in its present form.

Finally, thanks to my mother and brother—and other relatives I name or describe here—for their love and all they have done for me over the years. They never anticipated appearing in my essays; I hope the total results do not displease them.

THIS BOOK IS DEDICATED TO
THE BELOVED DEAD,

Matthew David Torgovnick

Salvatore De Marco, Sr.

Nathan Torgovnick

Victor Torgovnick

Richard Chernick

Note on the Author

MARIANNA DE MARCO TORGOVNICK, professor of English at Duke University, is the author of the acclaimed *Gone Primitive: Savage Intellects, Modern Lives,* also published by the University of Chicago Press. The first essay of this collection, "On Being White, Female, and Born in Bensonhurst," was selected for *Best American Essays, 1991.*